# BookMarks

## Volume 6

## Bible Explorations for Older Youth

### Edited by
### Sandra DeMott Hasenauer

**Judson Press ■ Valley Forge**

**BookMarks, Volume 6: Bible Explorations for Older Youth**

© 2002 by Judson Press, Valley Forge, PA 19482-0851

---

**Library of Congress Cataloging-in-Publication Data**

    (Revised for volume 6)

Bible explorations for older youth / edited by Sandra DeMott Hasenauer.

    p.   cm.

Volume 6: ISBN 0-8170-1419-5 (pbk. : alk. paper)

Volume 5: ISBN 0-8170-1418-7 (pbk. : alk. paper)

Volume 4: ISBN 0-8170-1334-2 (pbk. : alk. paper)

Volume 3: ISBN 0-8170-1333-4 (pbk. : alk. paper)

Volume 2: ISBN 0-8170-1332-6 (pbk. : alk. paper)

Volume 1: ISBN 0-8170-1331-8 (pbk. : alk. paper)

1. Bible–Study and teaching.   2. Christian education of young people.   I. Hasenauer, Sandra DeMott.  II. Series: Bookmarks (Judson Press) ; v. 6.

BS600.2.B443 1999

220'.071'2–dc21                                       99-36852

Printed in the U.S.A.

08  07  06  05  04  03  02

10  9  8  7  6  5  4  3  2  1

# Contents

Welcome to *BookMarks,* a fresh idea in Bible study curriculum for older youth. *BookMarks* combines a high regard for the biblical story with respect for the honesty and thoughtfulness of older youth. The sessions in this volume are specifically designed to give youth access to the Bible in a way that challenges youth to discover meaning in the Bible for their own lives. You'll notice the difference right away!

*BookMarks* is designed as an elective series for older youth, and may be used independently of other curricula or as a part of the larger curriculum series, *Bible Quest: A Bible Story Curriculum for All Ages,* with which it is affiliated. As part of the *Bible Quest* series, each volume of *BookMarks* will consider at least two of the four broad themes that emerge from the biblical story. These are: Covenant, Liberation and Justice, Salvation, and Incarnation. In addition, *BookMarks* sessions can easily be used in a number of Bible study settings, including Sunday school, youth group sessions, and retreats.

## The Story Is the Point

One of the greatest challenges for the church today is how to address the biblical illiteracy of young people who have grown up in the church. Many youth who have spent years in Sunday school and youth programs remember little about what is in the Bible. Although the Bible has been used to teach many lessons, youth seem to have missed the story behind the message—end of lesson, end of story! For *BookMarks,* the biblical story *is* the point! The objective of each session is to create an opportunity for youth to engage the story directly, so that the biblical story itself is what is remembered. Through this direct encounter with the Bible, the Bible story is joined to the story of our own lives, challenging our behavior, informing our decisions, and nurturing our relationship with God.

## The Learner Is an Interpreter

*BookMarks* values the perspectives youth bring to their study of the Bible. Each session encourages youth to see the biblical story in light of their own lives. In addition, each session provides an opportunity for youth to practice using tools and approaches that contribute to responsible interpretation. As youth become familiar with the process of biblical interpretation, they are encouraged to consider the Bible an accessible resource for faith and life. As youth are able to see the connections between their own story and the biblical story, they discover meaning in that story and learn to look to Scripture as a resource for living now and in the future.

## A Six-Step Process

The sessions in *BookMarks* use a six-step process to help youth engage the Bible story and find meaning in that story for their lives. Each step includes two options, so the leader can design the session especially for the needs of the youth. In "Setting the Stage," youth are welcomed into the interpretive process through activities and discussions that foreshadow key features of the story to be considered. In "Telling the Story," the story itself is presented in ways that will help youth to pay close attention to its plot, characters, and content. In "Reacting to the Story," youth are invited and helped to share their initial responses to the story, including their questions and their first impressions of its meaning. In "Connecting to the Story," youth are challenged to discover the intersection of the biblical story with their own lives, seeing themselves through the characters and situations of the Bible story and beginning to identify the personal relevance of the story. In "Exploring the Story," youth are introduced to various tools and approaches for responsible biblical interpretation, encouraging them to place their own understanding of the story in the context of the wider faith community. In "Living the Story," youth express their emerging sense of the meaning of the story for their lives in a closing context of affirmation and worship. In addition, each *BookMarks* session includes two reproducible handouts designed to contribute to the learning process.

## Additional Features

In addition to the six-step process with two options in each step, *BookMarks* sessions include a number of other features to support the leader in the process of helping youth discover the relevance of Scripture for their lives. "A Story behind the Story" provides the leader with contextual information about the biblical story, describing important historical, cultural, and theological background to the story. "Possible Youth Contact Points" suggests some of the issues and questions important to youth that may become avenues of connection to the biblical story. "You May Need" provides an up-front look at the materials you may need to gather depending on the session options you choose. "Enter the Story" suggests a process for the leader's intentional engagement with the Bible story prior to leading the session, encouraging reflection that may contribute to the interpretive process. "Things to Ponder" helps the leader to be aware of possible issues for youth that may emerge or need further attention as a result of studying a particular Bible story. "Looking Ahead" helps the leader to anticipate those options in the next session that may need some extra preparation time.

## The Writers for This Volume

CAROL S. ADAMS, a newlywed, takes time away from her spouse to write. Together they enjoy working with youth, camping, and eating cookies.

SANDRA DEMOTT HASENAUER is an American Baptist minister living in Rochester, New York, and currently serving as associate executive director for American Baptist Women in Valley Forge, Pennsylvania. In addition to editing and writing for this volume, Sandra also edited Volumes 2, 4, and 6 of the *BookMarks* series.

PAUL MAST HEWITT has more than seven years of experience as minister to youth and children. Currently he serves as a family worker with Lifelink Head Start in West Chicago, Illinois.

CHRIS HOLLIDAY is associate pastor of the First Baptist Church of Penfield, New York. He enjoys writing, planning worship, praising God with music, and ministering to and with youth and children.

LISA HOLLIDAY is senior pastor of the First Baptist Church in Penfield, New York. Her experience in youth ministry includes local church leadership in Kansas and Illinois, and she has led regional and national Christian education workshops for youth events.

DOTTY LUERA is minister of Christian education and youth programs at First Christian Church of Richardson, Texas. She has written curriculum for camps and conferences of the North Texas area (Disciples of Christ) and lives in Corsicana, Texas, with her spouse, Mark.

MARK RAMBO is associate pastor of First Baptist Church in Olympia, Washington. In addition to his pastoral ministry, he contributes to the leadership of regional and national Christian education and youth ministry programs for the American Baptist Churches USA.

KAREN YEE is associate pastor of First Baptist Church of Alameda, California. In addition to her local church ministry, she contributes to the leadership of regional and national Christian education events associated with the American Baptist Churches USA and other ministry organizations.

It is my sincere hope that you and your youth will enjoy these sixteen sessions as a fresh opportunity to consider the biblical story as full of meaning for our lives.

Grace and peace to you in Christ,

*Sandra DeMott Hasenauer*

Sandra DeMott Hasenauer
American Baptist Women
American Baptist Churches USA

# 1. The Anointing of David

*Bible Story: 1 Samuel 16:1-13*

Lisa and Chris Holliday

## A Story behind the Story

Earlier in 1 Samuel, the Israelites asked God for a king. God granted their desire and had Samuel (judge, priest, and prophet) anoint Saul as king of Israel (1 Samuel 10:1). King Saul was not faithful to God, and God eventually regretted choosing him. In chapter 15, God rejected Saul as king.

As 1 Samuel 16 begins, Samuel is obviously grieving over God's rejection of Saul and Saul's unfaithfulness. God seems to rebuke Samuel, basically telling him that it's time to move on. God instructs Samuel to fill his horn with oil, go to Bethlehem, and find Jesse, for one of Jesse's sons will be the next king.

Saul's father was apparently wealthy and powerful (1 Samuel 9:1), but Jesse is not. Also, Jesse's ancestors do not fit the typical idea of a royal family. After all, his family tree includes an immigrant Moabite (Ruth), a woman accused of adultery (Tamar, in Genesis 38), and a prostitute (Rahab, in Joshua 2). Would Jesse's family raise up the next king? Normally, it would be unthinkable. However, God, as usual, is operating on a different set of priorities than those of society.

Samuel is afraid to go, for he fears Saul will find out what he's doing and kill him. God reassures Samuel by walking him through the entire process, telling him to take a heifer to sacrifice and to invite Jesse and his sons to the ritual. When Samuel, Jesse, and seven of Jesse's eight sons gather, Samuel instantly thinks that Eliab, the tall and strong eldest son, is the chosen one. After all, Eliab looks like a king, doesn't he? God sets Samuel straight, reminding him, "The LORD does not see as mortals see; they look on the outward appearance, but the LORD looks on the heart" (1 Samuel 16:7).

Then each son passes before Samuel, but not one of them is the chosen one. At a loss, Samuel asks (in so many words), "Is this it?" Well, no, as it turns out, there's still the baby of the family, David. He's out tending sheep. Samuel insists that David be sent for, and God tells Samuel that *this* son is the one. In other words, God turns the expectations of the world upside down by choosing the youngest son and by choosing a shepherd. Thus David becomes anointed as God's chosen king of Israel.

This story once again points out God's ability to turn our expectations on their ears—a story that foreshadows the gift of the only begotten Son many generations later to a young, unmarried peasant woman of the countryside.

## Enter the Story

Much occurs between the time of David's secret anointing by Samuel and his public anointings. Read 1 Samuel 8:1–2 Samuel 5:5 to better comprehend the flow of events and the circumstances surrounding David's ascent to the throne. A Bible with section titles will be most useful for this exercise.

## POSSIBLE YOUTH CONTACT POINTS

- **What does God want me to do with my life?**
- **Does God have a special calling for me?**
- **What does God see when God looks at my heart?**
- **What do I see when I look in the mirror?**
- **Do I see others the way God sees them?**
- **How can I "be me" in a society that values appearances over what's inside?**

## YOU MAY NEED

- **Bibles**
- **newsprint and markers**
- **writing utensils**
- **paper**
- **thin markers**
- **one wrapped gift per youth**
- **strips of paper (with a number written on each)**
- **container**
- **strips of paper with characters' names or descriptions**
- **pictures of five very different-looking people whom the youth don't know**
- **video camera, blank tape (optional)**
- **costumes and props (optional)**
- **computers (optional)**
- **"What Ya Thinkin'?" handouts**
- **videotape of commercials and a brief video clip of a reality TV program (such as *Survivor* or *The Real World*)**
- **TV and VCR**
- **"God Vision" handouts**
- **Bible study resources, such as concordances, study Bibles, Bible dictionaries and encyclopedias, commentaries on 1 Samuel, etc.**
- **guest speaker who knows about sheep and shepherds**

*Continued on page 3 . . .*

Also, take some time to consider why God chose David. What did God see in David's heart? What were David's talents and skills? Describe his character. Now, take time to consider what God sees when God looks at your own heart. Who are you underneath it all? When you look in the mirror, what do you see?

As you know, youth particularly struggle with identity and image. So much of the culture tells them that their outer appearance matters most. They long for acceptance and will sometimes go to unhealthy extremes to find it. Spend some time praying for the youth to whom and with whom you minister. Ask God to guide you in your efforts to help the youth value what God values: what's inside.

## Setting the Stage (5–10 minutes)

### OPTION A

*Needed: one wrapped gift per youth, strips of paper, container*
Before the session, prepare one gift per youth. Choose gift boxes that are a lot of different sizes and shapes and decorate them in a variety of ways. Some boxes should look plain or unattractive, while others should look exciting or interesting. Some gifts should be things the youth want (candy, snack food, money), while others should be things they do not want (twigs, spoiled food, a penny). You could even go to extremes on a few good gifts and give a CD or movie gift certificate. Make sure some (but not all) of the best gifts are in unattractive packages and some (but not all) of the worst gifts are in attractive packages. Also, create as many

numbered slips of paper as you have youth; fold the papers and put them in a container.

As the youth enter the room, tell them they will soon get to choose a gift. Invite them to look at, but not touch, the gifts. Once everyone has arrived, have each youth draw a number from the basket. Allow the person with the highest number to select the first gift. Then the person with the second-highest number goes, and so on. Everyone must select a gift by sight only. Once they choose, hand them the gift. After everyone has a gift, go around the room and let one person at a time open his or her gift.

Once all the gifts are open, ask the group:

- Why did you choose the gifts you did?
- Did the outside of your gift match what was on the inside? How or how not?
- Is what's on the outside a good indicator of what's on the inside?

### OPTION B

*Needed: pictures of five very different-looking people whom the youth don't know*
Tell the group that you are going to show them pictures of five different people. As you show them each picture, invite the youth to describe that person as best they can.

Once the youth have finished describing all five people, ask:

- Do we know any of these people?
- What did we base our descriptions upon?
- Is it possible that some of our ideas about this person are incorrect?
- Is what's on the outside a good indicator of what's on the inside?

■ Does our society categorize people more by their outsides or their insides?

Let the youth know that today's story tells about someone who is judged by the outside and the inside in different ways.

## Telling the Story
### (5–10 minutes)
OPTION A
*Needed: Bibles, costumes and props (optional), video camera, blank tape, and TV with VCR (optional)*
Divide the large group into at least two smaller groups. Ask the groups to read 1 Samuel 16:1-13 in their groups and then prepare a skit of the story. Invite them to consider all the characters, including God, Samuel, the calf, the elders of Bethlehem, Jesse, David's seven older brothers (three of whom are mentioned by name: Eliab, Abinadab, Shammah), and David. They could also have a narrator, if they wish. If you have access to costumes and props, let the youth choose what they want. This will greatly add to the fun.

Once the groups have had adequate time to prepare, gather the youth together and invite each group to perform their skit. Conclude this section by having someone read the Scripture passage out loud while the youth follow along in their Bibles. If you have the time, equipment, and capabilities, videotape the skits and allow the youth to watch themselves in action.

OPTION B
*Needed: Bibles, strips of paper with characters' names or descriptions, container, newsprint, markers*
Before the session, write each story character's name or description on a strip of paper and then fold it so the name is not visible. (The characters are listed in "Telling the Story," Option A.) Put the strips of paper in a container and have them available for this session.

Have some of the youth read 1 Samuel 16:1-13 out loud to the group. When they are finished, ask the group to list all the characters in the story. Write the characters' names on newsprint. Tell the youth that you are going to pass a container around and that each strip of paper contains a character's name or description. Ask the youth to take a strip of paper out of the basket, but ask them not to share the name on it with anyone else. After everyone has one, tell the youth that you are going to read the Scripture passage again. As you do, ask the youth to put themselves into their character's mind and to consider what that character may have been thinking or feeling. Also ask them to think about what their character may have been feeling toward other characters. Read the Scripture out loud once or twice to give the youth time to get into the character and think about the possibilities.

## Reacting to the Story
### (15–20 minutes)
OPTION A
*Needed: Bibles, regular markers, thin markers, newsprint, computers (optional)*
Divide the group into pairs or small groups and ask them to take their Bibles. Give each pair a piece of newsprint and some thin and thick markers. Ask them to create a front page headline and an article for *The Bethlehem Times* concerning the events in 1 Samuel 16:1-13. Ask

■ W. Phillip Keller's *A Shepherd Looks at Psalm 23* (Zondervan, 1997) or *Lessons from a Sheep Dog* (Word, 1988)
■ newsprint prepared with questions from "Living the Story," Option A
■ newsprint prepared with questions from "Living the Story," Option B
■ closing song

3

them to be specific about the facts and also to offer some opinions and commentary. Encourage them to include interviews with the characters and to draw pictures within the text of the article. Tell them they can fold or adapt the newsprint in any way they wish. Have more newsprint available if they need it.

Once each pair has completed their project, gather the large group together. Spend some time sharing everyone's work with the rest of the group, and be sure to congratulate everyone's efforts. Consider posting the newspaper articles someplace where the whole church could appreciate them.

If you have access to enough computers, let the pairs create their articles using a desktop publishing program as an alternative to the newsprint.

OPTION B
*(This option follows Option B of "Telling the Story.")*
*Needed: Bibles, writing utensils, "What Ya Thinkin'?" handouts, colored pencils, thin markers, or crayons*
Tell the youth that it is helpful to attempt to understand each character's perspective when studying the Bible. Spend a moment discussing the way our perspectives change depending on who we are in a given situation. Sometimes we are the Davids; sometimes, the Samuels.

Give each youth a "What Ya Thinkin'?" handout and a pencil. Ask them to find a quiet place apart from the others to continue reflecting on their characters. Invite the youth to complete Part A of the handout and to use a Bible to

reread the Scripture passage if needed. Ask them to somehow represent what they believe their character thought or felt throughout the story, including how he felt about the other characters and about God. They could draw pictures or symbols, write down their thoughts, create a graph or chart—whatever works for them. After everyone has finished Part A, gather the large group and have each youth share his or her response.

Now that the youth have had time to consider all the characters together, ask everyone to answer Part B of the handout as themselves, not as their characters. Invite those who wish to share these responses with the group to do so.

## Connecting to the Story (15–20 minutes)
OPTION A
*Needed: Bible, videotape of commercials and a clip of a reality TV program, TV and VCR*
Before the session, videotape a few commercials that rely on appearance and image to sell their product. Also videotape a clip of a reality TV show.

Show the commercials. Ask the youth what was used to sell each product (sex, image, power, fame, coolness). Ask:
■ Why do you think our culture is so caught up in outward appearances?
■ What does 1 Samuel 16:7 say that God sees when God looks at us?
■ What is the "heart" of a person?
■ Why doesn't our society look at the "heart" of people more?

Then show a clip of a reality TV program. Ask:

4

■ Why do you think our culture has been so interested in reality TV programs lately?

■ Do people *really* want to know another person's true self?

■ Do they want to know if the person is nice or mean, devoted or unfaithful?

Divide the group into at least two groups. Ask each group to create a reality TV show that is interested in the inside reality more than outside appearance. Invite them to create a three-minute reality TV skit that centers on getting to know the heart of a person. After they've had time to prepare, ask them to present their skits. After each skit, allow the large group to ask questions of the performers and discuss the skit.

OPTION B
*Needed: Bible, "God Vision" handouts, writing utensils*
Read 1 Samuel 16:7 out loud to the youth. Ask the youth:

■ What did Samuel see when he looked at David?

■ What do you think David saw when he looked at his own reflection?

■ What did God see when God looked at David?

Give each youth a "God Vision" handout and a writing utensil. Ask the youth to write a description of their outer selves all around the outside of the body outline on the handout. Then invite them to write in the heart what they think God sees when God looks at them. Have several mirrors available, small or large, and encourage students to look at themselves from time to time while working on the handout.

Once the youth have completed the handout, ask them to find a friend with whom they can share some of what they've written. Encourage the youth to be affirming and respectful of each other during this time of intimate sharing.

## Exploring the Story
### (15–20 minutes)
OPTION A
*Needed: Bibles, Bible study resources, paper, writing utensils*
Say something like: *In 1 Samuel 13:14, Samuel tells King Saul, "Your kingdom will not continue; the LORD has sought out a man after his own heart; and the LORD has appointed him to be ruler over his people, because you have not kept what the LORD commanded you." In this story, that man was David. Let's explore David's life, his talents and gifts, and his important role in the story of God's people.*

Divide the youth into at least two groups. Give them paper and something to write with and make Bible study resources available. Invite one group to make a time line of major events that were somehow associated with David. Have them start at his anointing in 1 Samuel 16 and go all the way to the birth of Jesus in Matthew 1. Have the second group make a list of David's talents, gifts, and qualities evident in the various stories associated with him. Have both groups explore David's faithfulness as well as his unfaithfulness.

After the groups are finished, gather everyone together and have a time of sharing. Ask:

■ What are some mistakes that David made?

5

- What are some of his poorer qualities?
- What are some of his better qualities?
- Would you say that David is a man after God's own heart? Why or why not?
- How did God make use of David?

OPTION B
*Needed: guest speaker, Phillip Keller books (optional)*
Invite a guest speaker who knows something about shepherds and sheep, particularly those in Old Testament times. A real shepherd, a pastor, or another person who has researched this topic would work well. Two books by Phillip Keller, *A Shepherd Looks at Psalm 23* and *Lessons from a Sheep Dog*, would be wonderful resources for the special guest. Have the speaker present information and stories about the job of a shepherd (especially in David's time) and about the kind of heart a shepherd must have to properly care for and protect sheep.

After the guest's brief presentation, ask the youth:
- What is the significance of David's being a shepherd?
- Are there other famous figures in the Bible who are called shepherds?
- Why do you think God picked a shepherd to be king?
- Was this in any way a foreshadowing of the type of king Jesus would be? Why or why not?
- Why is Jesus referred to as a shepherd?
- Why is Jesus referred to as a servant king?

## Living the Story
## (5–10 minutes)
OPTION A
*(This option follows Option B of "Connecting to the Story.")*
*Needed: newsprint prepared with questions below, "God Vision" handouts, writing utensils, paper, closing song*
Before the session, write the following questions on newsprint:
- What are your talents and strengths, and how can you use them to serve God and your neighbors near and far?
- What type of person is God calling you to be?
- What do you think God wants you to do this year?
- What do you think God is calling you to do with your life?

Talk with the youth about Samuel's and David's callings. Also, talk about your own calling or use other modern-day examples. Now ask the youth to use their "God Vision" handouts and the newsprint questions to help them assess their hearts and their callings in life. Of course, parts of a person's calling may change over the years, but right now, what do they hear God saying to them about their immediate and long-term futures?

After the group has had time to reflect and write about this, gather them together in a circle and have the youth each share one thing they believe God is calling them to do or be. Then sing a hymn of commitment, such as "Make Me a Servant," "Come, All Christians, Be Committed," or "Here I Am, Lord." End with a closing prayer and pray for the youth, their lives, and their callings.

OPTION B
*Needed: newsprint, markers, newsprint prepared with questions below, closing song*
Before the session, list these questions on newsprint:
■ What is our calling or purpose as a youth group?
■ What can we do to get to know the hearts of people instead of judging them by their appearances?
■ How can our youth group be shepherds for those who need to be found?
■ How can we care for and serve others?

Help the youth create a group service project that corresponds to some of the issues this session has brought up. Write the group's ideas on newsprint. Help them find the information they need to plan the project and set a date for it as soon as possible. For example, the group could serve a meal at a homeless shelter or transitional home and also spend time talking with the people. Maybe some youth could sing or perform for the people partaking in the meal, make cards for them, etc. Encourage your youth's ideas and affirm their willingness to be servants.

Sing a hymn of commitment, such as "Make Me a Servant," "Come, All Christians, Be Committed," or "Here I Am, Lord." End with a closing prayer and pray for the youth and the service project the group is planning.

**Things to Ponder**
This session may have highlighted several sensitive issues for the youth. Several may be struggling with what God wants them to do with their lives, especially the juniors and seniors. Many may be tired of being judged by their appearances, and they may long to better know their own hearts. Let the youth know that you are available to talk with them about their lives. Perhaps you could offer yourself for after-school coffee or soda appointments with the youth. Take time this week to thank God for each youth and for who each is.

**Looking Ahead**
For Session 2, you may need to find a video of the film *Godspell*, two adult volunteers, and a contemporary Christian music CD. Be sure to read through the session to give yourself enough time to prepare. Be sure to look through all the sessions you will be teaching—some of them may require advance preparation. Session 7 has, as Option A of "Living the Story," the possibility of painting a large wall mural based on the Creation story. You will want to read through this option now in order to prepare and schedule enough time for its completion.

# What Ya Thinkin'?

**Part A**

My character's name or description: _____

Express what you believe the character thought or felt throughout the story, including how he felt about the other characters and toward God. You could draw pictures or symbols, write your thoughts, create a graph or chart, etc.

**Part B**

Of all the characters in the story, I identify most with _____

because _____

_____

_____

_____

_____ .

## God Vision

*"The LORD does not see as mortals see; they look on the outward appearance, but the LORD looks on the heart."*—1 Samuel 16:7

# 2. Jesus' Baptism

*Bible Story: Mark 1:1-11*

Mark Rambo

## A Story behind the Story

"The beginning of the good news of Jesus Christ, the Son of God" (Mark 1:1). These few words mark the start of what might have been a turning point in Christian history: the first attempt to put faith in Christ into the written word. So few words, actually, but they hint at such a deep relationship. It's as if the Gospel writer were saying, "Here is the news of our Savior. Sit awhile and read, why don't you? Share in the experience of Jesus that I have had. Make these stories your own."

Mark's Gospel is generally accepted as the earliest written of the four New Testament Gospels. It also happens to be the shortest. There is not a lot of in-depth analysis of the stories. Rather, the writer of Mark gets right to the heart of the matter. He is very concise. It is sometimes assumed that, since this is the first Gospel, the writer's main concern is to get the stories down so that they can be shared with a wider audience than what the previous oral tradition had allowed. Mark is all about the stories of Jesus, sharing his life with the world.

The author starts Jesus' story in a rather unusual way compared to the other Gospel writers. Rather than beginning with a birth narrative, this Gospel begins with the activity of John the Baptist. Because of this, the concept of our preparation to enter God's reign is an area that can be meaningfully explored during this lesson. Think of who was instrumental in preparing you to be a part of God's reign. Who prayed for you? Who shared the gospel with you? Who played a significant role in your Christian experience?

Another thing to ponder as you explore this text is that many of us come from different faith experiences. Your group might have a mix of those who were baptized as infants and those who were baptized when they were older. Remember, too, that whatever we have experienced, whatever our own understandings of baptism are, there will be some young people who have different understandings or none at all. Be prepared for those types of questions or situations to arise.

But, as in all of our dealings with Scripture, we must look at these words as shedding light on our own relationship with Jesus Christ and our own attempts to follow his teachings. Can our lives be evidence of "the good news of Jesus Christ, the Son of God"?

## Enter the Story

Find a quiet place where there can be no interruptions for ten minutes. Start with prayer, as you seek God's Spirit to bring clarity, wisdom, and insight to the text. If you are very familiar with this passage, pray for new understandings.

Read the narrative for the first time. After you have read the text, pray again. Once you have prayed, read the passage again. This time write down some notes. What questions do you have? What impressions do you have of, or what reactions do you have to, the story you have just read and prayed over? After you have done this, think of your young people. Who has been baptized? Who has not? Do you even know who has or has not been baptized? Pray for your youth.

It may be helpful for you to read the other Gospel accounts of Jesus' baptism as well as their accounts of John the Baptist. It would helpful to immerse yourself, if you will, in these other texts from Matthew, Luke, and John. Think of your own baptism or confirmation experience. Draw from it as you enter the story. Your personal recollections will be important for the youth.

**Setting the Stage
(5–10 minutes)**
OPTION A
*Needed: writing utensils, index cards*
Once everyone has arrived, allow some time to talk about the past week, perhaps by going around the class and asking the youth to share one high and one low from the past few days. Close this time of sharing with a prayer. Then hand out a writing utensil and index card to each youth.

Invite the youth to write down the names of people who made their first week of high school bearable. Who made them comfortable? Who helped them get ready for what high school would be like? After they have jotted down the

names, go around the group and ask for volunteers to share the names they wrote. Discuss:

- What did these people say to help you get ready?
- How did they help?
- What was it that they did that made a difference for you that first week?

After this time of sharing, let the youth know that this session's Bible story is about a time of preparation.

OPTION B
*Needed: TV and VCR, video of* Godspell, *snack*
Ahead of time, cue the movie to the opening scene including the song "Prepare Ye the Way of the Lord."

Welcome the youth as they enter and spend some time checking in on their week. Be sure that everyone has an opportunity to check in. After you have done that, share with the youth that they will be seeing a brief clip from a movie on the life of Jesus. Don't share anything else about the movie, not even the title.

Before you view the clip, divide the youth into pairs or triads, depending on the size of your group, and have them share about their hardest test at school. What made it hard? How did they study for it? How did they get ready for the test?

After they have had time to share, introduce the video clip without any fanfare. Try to position yourself to watch their faces as they view the clip. Share the snack while you watch.

Once the clip is over, ask each person to share one reaction to

**POSSIBLE YOUTH CONTACT POINTS**

- Who do I know who needs new life?
- Who do I know who needs to hear God's words of acceptance?
- Can I really be forgiven?
- Can I trust God's words?
- What in my life needs changing?

**YOU MAY NEED**

- writing utensils
- index cards (for two different options)
- TV and VCR
- video of *Godspell,* cued to "Prepare Ye the Way of the Lord"[1]
- snack of some kind
- newsprint and markers
- at least one copy of *The Message* (Eugene Peterson, NavPress, 2000) or another contemporary paraphrase of the Bible
- Bibles
- "You are There" handouts
- two adult volunteers (preferably one baptized as a youth and a second baptized as an adult) to share their baptism experiences with the class
- paper
- CD player and some favorite Christian CDs
- newsprint prepared with questions as listed in Option B of "Connecting to the Story"
- "Compare and Contrast" handouts
- tempera paint, butcher paper (or other paper suitable for painting), and paintbrushes, *or* finger paints, finger painting or freezer paper, and access to a sink for washing hands
- Christian song on CD that fits the theme of baptism or commitments of faith *or* quiet meditative music[2]

what they have just witnessed. Ask them what the clip was about. See if they recognized what Bible account was being played out on the screen. To end the discussion, mention that today's story is about Jesus' baptism, and invite the youth to prepare to hear that story.

## Telling the Story (5–10 minutes)
OPTION A
*Needed: newsprint, marker, Bibles,* **The Message** *or other contemporary paraphrase*
Make sure everyone has a Bible and invite them to find Mark 1:1-11. Read the passage in a way that best fits your group, whether that is one person reading out loud or alternating readers one verse at a time. After reading the story, take your marker and newsprint and have the youth shout out what they just heard. What were their impressions? What questions did the story raise for them? What did they see in their mind's eye as they heard the story read?

After you have written down their initial responses to the story, read it again. This time, read it from a contemporary paraphrase such as *The Message*. Have the youth close their eyes and pretend that they are witnesses to what they are about to hear. You are asking them to place themselves within the story. After the story has been told this second time, ask the youth to share what they "saw" as the story was read. Have them consider what they might have heard, smelled, or felt, had they been present during the events. Record their responses on the same newsprint.

OPTION B
*Needed: "You are There" handouts, writing utensils, Bibles,* **The Message** *or similar contemporary paraphrase*
Read out loud Mark 1:1-11. You may read this in whatever fashion is most comfortable for your group. Some like just one reader; others like to share the reading load.

After the story has been read the first time, pass out copies of the "You Are There" handout along with writing utensils. Explain to the youth that this time you will read the story from *The Message* (or whatever paraphrase you have chosen). Invite the youth to put themselves into the story. They are to think of themselves as eyewitnesses to what they are hearing. After everyone has their handout, have them close their eyes and hear the story again from *The Message*. After the reading, allow sufficient time for the youth to work on their handouts.

## Reacting to the Story (15–20 minutes)
OPTION A
*(This option follows Option A of "Telling the Story.")*
*Needed: newsprint and markers*
Break your youth into smaller groups of about three or four youth per group. Invite the youth to imagine that they are journalists from the time of Jesus. If you are feeling especially creative, have one or more groups imagine themselves as Roman journalists (reminding the youth that the Romans were the occupying force of the time), another group imagine themselves as Hebrew journalists, and a third

group or more imagine themselves as journalists who are going to end up among the first disciples of Jesus (in other words, who might have a distinctly Christian outlook). Instruct the groups to take newsprint and markers and come up with a newspaper headline based upon the story they just heard read. If you've assigned particular cultural roles, they may need to take a few moments to imagine how that might change their outlook on the story. Give them time to create a rough draft as well as their final product.

After they have completed their newspaper headlines, have each group share their creations with the rest of the class. They should give an explanation as to the reasoning behind the headline and how it reflects the story.

OPTION B
*(This option follows Option B of "Telling the Story.")*
*Needed: "You Are There" hand-outs, newsprint and markers*
Break the youth into pairs or triads, and have them share with each other their responses to the questions on the "You Are There" handout. Give them adequate time for sharing, but keep them moving and on task.

After a reasonable time, have the groups share their responses with the larger group, one at a time. Do not allow other groups to respond to the reporting group at this time—there will be time allotted for that at the end of the exercise. On newsprint, record each group's discoveries as they are shared. After every group has had a chance to

report, invite the entire class to see what commonalities there are among the items recorded on newsprint. What are the differences? Affirm the good work that the youth have done as "eyewitnesses" to the story.

## Connecting to the Story (15–20 minutes)
OPTION A
*Needed: two adult volunteers to share their baptism or confirmation experiences, paper, writing utensils*
Have two folks from the church come in to share their stories of baptism or confirmation. Invite them to speak about the people who had an impact on their faith journey, which led to baptism or confirmation. What did those persons do that had impact? Was it their words or how they lived their life? You also will want them to describe their actual baptism if they were baptized as youth or adults. What did it feel like? Where did it take place? What emotions did they experience?

After each volunteer has had an opportunity to tell his or her story, you can now have the youth ask any questions they might have of the volunteers. (After this, the volunteers may leave, if they choose.) Hand out paper and writing utensils and have the youth reflect and write down their responses to what they have heard. Possible questions you may have them reflect on could include the following:
■ How was the person's story of baptism or confirmation similar to your own?
■ If you have not been baptized yet, how did the story make you feel?

■ Does it help you get a sense of what Jesus might have experienced with his own baptism? If so, why?

After you have given the youth time to work through this exercise, return to the larger group and have those who are willing share their reflections.

OPTION B
*Needed: CD player, some favorite Christian CDs, newsprint prepared with the questions below, newsprint and marker, paper, writing utensils*
This option gives you the opportunity to share your own spiritual journey that led to your baptism or confirmation. Whether you were a young child or an adult, circumstances within your life led to your decision. Share from your heart; youth respond to openness and honesty. And after you have shared with them, allow some time for them to ask you questions. Be sensitive to their questions—you never know what they are processing inside themselves.

After you have processed your story with them, post newsprint prepared with the following questions:
■ Who has had the most influence on you so far?
■ Who influences you the most at school?
■ Who influences you the most at church?
■ Who has prepared you for life so far?
■ How has that person prepared you?
Pass out paper and writing utensils and have the youth write down their responses to the questions. You may want to play some music while they are working. After an adequate time frame, have the youth share their responses in pairs. When everyone has shared, bring the group back together and ask for volunteers to share their response to any of the questions.

**Exploring the Story (15–20 minutes)**
OPTION A
*Needed: "Compare and Contrast" handouts, writing utensils, Bibles*
Pass out copies of the "Compare and Contrast" handouts. This handout will have the youth comparing and contrasting the other Gospel accounts of John the Baptist and Jesus' baptism. Note that the Gospel of John is extremely different from Matthew and Luke. It's important that the youth begin exploring these differences among the Gospel writers, as well as their similarities.

Make sure that each youth now has a Bible, a pen or pencil, and the handout. Break the overall group into groups of three or whatever is appropriate for your setting. Have them explore the different accounts as well as respond to the questions on the handout.

After they have completed the biblical exploration, have the group share their findings. For those people who have chosen a story with which they connect the most, have them choose one verse from that story that they particularly like. Once they've done so, invite them to write that verse on the back of their handout, perhaps even taking a moment or two to decorate the verse in some way. Encourage them to memorize their verse, so that they will have it to draw upon in times of trouble or sadness throughout their life.

OPTION B
*Needed: tempera paint, butcher paper, and paintbrushes,* or *finger paints, finger-paint paper or freezer paper, and access to a sink for washing hands, Bibles*
Divide the youth into four teams (a team can be one person). Each team will be given a different account of Jesus' baptism. Assign each group one of the following:
■ Mark 1:1-11
■ Matthew 3:1-17
■ Luke 3:1-22
■ John 1:19-34

Once the group has been given their story, have them go over the story together. Their task is to recreate the story they have read using pictures, symbols, words, etc. Make sure each group has the painting supplies of your choice so they can create their renderings of the Gospel stories.

After they are done with their artistic creations, display the stories and have each group share about their works of art. And then, once every group has finished sharing, go over with the entire group the similarities and differences among the stories as are reflected in their drawings.

**Living the Story
(5–10 minutes)**
OPTION A
*Needed: CD player and appropriate Christian song on CD (optional)*
Gather the participants into a circle and thank them for all of their good

work. If any seemed to take an extra risk in their participation, acknowledge that. However, be sure to spread the praise around to everyone. Also, encourage the youth to thank the adult volunteers (if you used that option) next time they see them.

Have the group close their eyes. If you desire, play your chosen song and invite the youth to quietly reflect on the lyrics. After the song is over, encourage the youth to remain quiet and reflective as you retell the story of Jesus' baptism from Mark in your own words. Whisper gently the last part where God speaks directly to Jesus. While their eyes are still closed, remind them that whether they have been baptized or not, God's love is whispering to each of them, "You are my child, in whom I am well pleased." Let that linger for a few seconds and then close your time with prayer.

OPTION B
*Needed: index cards, writing utensils*
Gather the group together in a circle. Make sure to praise them for all of their good work during this process. Make sure you spread the praise around for everyone, not just one or two. Invite some last questions or shared reflections on the Bible story itself, and spend a moment or two to review together what you accomplished during the session.

After you've taken some time to look at the last hour or so you've spent together, pass out the writing utensils and index cards. Remind the youth of the words that God spoke to Jesus in Mark 1:11: "You are my child, in whom I am well pleased" (paraphrased). Ask the youth to take a moment and write down the names of two friends who need to hear God's word of love. If youth feel that they themselves particularly need to hear that word, they should feel free to write their own names on their cards. The cards will be kept private.

After the youth have written down their responses, encourage them to take the index card home and to pray for those two people at least once a day for a month. Offer a closing prayer asking God's Spirit to touch the lives of the youth in the circle as well as their friends whose names they have written down.

## Things to Ponder

You may or may not know who within the group has been baptized or confirmed. Make sure that throughout this learning process the young people do not feel manipulated if they have not yet been baptized or confirmed. Remember that, though acts of commitment are important, it is the Holy Spirit's job—not ours—to convict one's heart. Just remember to be sensitive.

## Looking Ahead

Several options in the next session require preparation, so be sure to provide yourself with plenty of time to prepare. Particularly, you may want to do a little research on the Gospels as described in the session.

## Notes

1. *Godspell* (Columbia TriStar Pictures, original release date 1973, rereleased 2000) is available in video and DVD formats through common bookstore Web sites. Invite the youth to look beyond the now somewhat dated 1970s appearance of the cast and choreography—the message and music are still wonderful! Explore whether there are any productions of *Godspell* in your area at this time; colleges often put this play on, updating it for the times.
2. Examples of a variety of musical styles include "Let it Rain" (Newsboys, *Going Public*, Starsong, 1995), "In Your Grace" (Kirk Franklin and 1NC, *1NC* [One Nation Crew], B-Rite, 2000), "The Vow" (Geoff Moore and the Distance, *Home Run!* Forefront, 1995), "Breathe" (*Hungry [Falling on My Knees]*, Vineyard, 1999). Note: If you choose "In Your Grace," you will need to decide whether you will play the spoken parts that are included in the music or stop and start right around the music itself.

# You Are There

*Using your imagination, put yourself out there in the desert with John the Baptist and Jesus. Take a moment to jot down what you see as an eyewitness.*

## Describe this man they call John the Baptist:

- What does he look like?

- How does he sound when he speaks?

- How does the crowd respond to him?

## Describe Jesus:

- What does he look like?

- How does Jesus look when he comes out of the water?

- What do you hear?

# Compare and Contrast

*Within your group, read, compare, and contrast the following stories:*

- **Mark 1:1-11**

- **Matthew 3:1-17**

- **Luke 3:1-22**

- **John 1:19-34**

Which characters within the stories are the same?

Which are different?

What are the overall similarities, if any, of the stories?

What are the overall differences?

Which story do you connect with the most, and why?

Which story do you connect with the least, and why?

# 3. Jesus' Resurrection

*Bible Story: John 20:1-18*

Mark Rambo

## A Story behind the Story

As the fourth Gospel, John's account resembles the other three in a general way, but it contains many stories of Jesus not found in the other books. This is also true when it comes to the story of Jesus and the resurrection. The resurrection is *the* event of our faith, separating us from other faith systems. Every person who has confessed Jesus as Lord and Savior knows the resurrection story intimately, yet it is a story—like many stories in our faith—that gets put on the shelf as if it were an old book. We bring it down once a year at Easter time, blow off the dust and cobwebs, hear it read to us, and then immediately place it back on the shelf for another year.

The resurrection account in John focuses on three witnesses to the empty tomb: Mary Magdalene, Peter, and a disciple who is described as "the other disciple" or "the disciple whom Jesus loved." Note that this "other disciple," as so described, is unique to John's Gospel. Some scholars identify this disciple as John (and assume him to be the Gospel writer), but there is no evidence that this assumption is true. Of the three witnesses mentioned above, only Mary Magdalene is mentioned by name in all four Gospels as an eyewitness to the empty tomb. She is also the first to actually see the resurrected Jesus in this account, and therefore she is the first to make that life-changing statement, "I have seen the Lord" (John 20:18).

The Gospel of John, as a whole, seems more concerned with the symbolic meaning of Jesus than with providing the readers and hearers of this word with information about what Jesus did and said. The symbolism the author uses comes from common experiences of the day. Terms such as "light," "bread," "water," "life," "door," etc., are used to enhance the significance of Jesus the Logos—the Word—who came to walk the streets of our lives with us. This is the story of the one who moves into the hearts of those who have experienced and believed the reality of God in their midst.

## Enter the Story

Though you are probably quite familiar with this story, it is important that you not give it a brief glance before you meet with your young people. Though each of the four Gospels has a resurrection story, each is unique and different from the others. Begin by finding a quiet place and praying—always the starting place when one prepares to engage the biblical story. Pray that a new thought or understanding may come out of your interaction with the text. Focus your prayer on your young people as well, both individually and as a group. Pray that all of you can enter the story with a sense of anticipation and excitement.

Read through the story and let it sink in. Let your thoughts stay

- Is it hard to believe in the resurrection?
- Would people believe me if I made a claim that someone who had died was no longer dead?
- Would I have the courage to make such a claim?
- Can I stand up for my faith when others question it?

## YOU MAY NEED

- snacks
- CD player and contemporary Christian music CDs
- tickets with numbers on them (one ticket per youth, numbered consecutively)
- three gift-wrapped boxes—two of them containing prizes (as described below) and the third empty
- three prizes—two of them wrapped in boxes (as described above) and the third concealed somewhere in the classroom[1]
- bandannas for each of the youth
- Bibles
- at least one copy of a contemporary paraphrase Bible, such as *The Message* (Eugene Peterson, NavPress, 2000)
- candle
- matches or lighter
- newsprint and markers
- paper
- writing utensils
- one large roll of white paper
- tempera paint and brushes
- "Witness" handouts
- "The Story of the Resurrection" handouts
- information on the four Gospels[2]
- Bible study helps, such as Bible dictionaries, Bible encyclopedias, commentaries, etc.

*Continued on page 21 . . .*

focused on what you have just read and let the words make a connection in you. Read the story again, but this time write down reactions or questions you have about this story. Since each of the Gospels has a resurrection story, consider reading each of them. What are their similarities? What are their differences? How do you give witness to your faith? What part of your faith is hard to believe?

## Setting the Stage (5–10 minutes)

Start your time together by welcoming the youth as they arrive. It can help make the youth look forward to attending class if you set the mood of a party as they enter. Having some good, upbeat Christian music playing at a moderate volume in the background will help make them feel at home. Even if your youth are not accustomed to listening to Christian music, sometimes they're surprised by the variety of music styles that are available now. Take the time to do some research yourself!

## OPTION A

*Needed: snacks, contemporary Christian music CD and CD player (optional)*

Once everyone has settled in with his or her food, go around and have the youth share one high and one low from the past week. Remember, not everyone has to share; they may pass if they wish. But encourage everyone to share at least one thing from their week. Remember to model this activity by including your own highs and lows.

After everyone has shared, offer up a prayer that reflects the sharing that has been done.

## OPTION B

*Needed: tickets with numbers on them, three gift-wrapped boxes, the third prize (unwrapped and concealed somewhere)*

After everyone has settled in with their snacks, pass out tickets for each youth present. Explain that today you will be "raffling off" three prizes because the youth have been such a joy to be with (or whatever reason you choose). Read off the first two prize numbers and let the winners receive their prizes. Save the largest, empty box for last.

After the first two prizes have been given away, draw the third number with a great flourish. Build up the anticipation for the drawing by saying that you've saved the best prize for last. Hand the prize to the winning youth, and watch for his or her reaction as well as the reactions of the other young people in the class. Obviously there will be shock and disappointment at what is *not* present. There will also be some smirks and possible laughter.

Ask the young person who "won" the last box how he or she felt upon seeing that the box was empty. Was this youth surprised? Mad? Confused? After he or she has answered your questions, give this youth the third prize, which you've concealed, and thank him or her for participating.

Let the young people know that today they will be hearing the story of the resurrection and the empty tomb. Explain that there were many different stories and reactions surrounding this empty tomb by Christians and non-Christians alike.

## Telling the Story
### (5–10 minutes)
OPTION A

*Needed: bandannas for each of the youth, Bibles, a contemporary paraphrase such as* The Message

Give participants a bandanna for covering their eyes, and invite the youth to spread out and find a quiet place apart from each other. Once they have found their place, have them place the bandanna over their eyes. When their eyes are covered, explain that you will read them today's story. Explain that near the end of the story you will pause and ask them to remove their blindfolds and then you will finish the story.

Begin reading the story slowly and reflectively. When you come to verse 15, slow down your reading even more. At verse 16, after saying Mary's name, pause and ask the youth to remove their bandannas but to remain quiet. Continue with the rest of the story.

After you have finished with the story, discuss the experience with questions like the following:
■ Was it hard for you to listen to the story blindfolded? Was it helpful? *in the dark*
■ When you removed the bandannas near the end of the story, did you hear what was happening within the story? Was it distracting or did it enhance the story?

Without the youth wearing their blindfolds, read the story again, but this time from your contemporary paraphrase.

OPTION B

*Needed: candle, matches or lighter, Bible*

Place a candle in a central location. Light the candle and dim the lights of your meeting space if you can. Explain that you are going to lead the class in a guided reflection related to today's story, from the perspective of one of its characters. Have the youth close their eyes, or invite them to stare into the candle.

Speak slowly and reflectively so that the learners can imagine themselves in the story: *Imagine you are outside. It is very early in the morning. The sun has yet to rise. Listen to the sounds of the early morning. What do you hear? Feel the morning air, cool and crisp as you slowly walk. Inhale. Exhale. A small cloud comes from your mouth. You are walking along a small path toward something, searching for something, numb from the cold, numb from life. Slowly shadows form as night gives way to the rising of the sun. As the sun comes slowly over the hill, you find that what you search for is gone. Panic! Where? Who has taken what you seek? Wait. Listen. More light. A sound. A light. A word. Mary! Teacher! Go, tell!*

Read John 18:1-11 slowly to finish the reflection.

## Reacting to the Story
### (15–20 minutes)
OPTION A

*Needed: newsprint and markers*

Post your newsprint and have the youth share their first impressions of what they have heard, as you serve as the group recorder. If the youth are hesitant, you may want

■ youth study Bible, such as *The Youth Bible* by Group Publishing (optional)[3]
■ praise song or hymn that your group knows (words written on newsprint or photocopies, if necessary)
■ musical accompanist, such as a guitarist or keyboard player
■ container big enough for burning paper (be sure to find a location for this activity that won't accidentally trigger smoke alarms)

to read the story one more time to help them process a response. You may want to ask questions as they share their initial responses to the story. What emotions did they hear or feel? What part of the story did they ignore? What part of the story drew or got their attention?

When you have completed your list of responses, divide the youth into pairs and have them focus on the emotions they heard or felt within the story. Make sure they can see the posted newsprint as a reference. Have the young people talk about times in their own lives when they experienced similar emotions or feelings. What was the situation they were facing when those emotions and feelings flowed through them? How was their situation similar or different to the story heard and read this session?

OPTION B
*Needed: paper, writing utensils, Bibles*
Give each of the youth paper and writing utensils. Make sure there are enough Bibles for everyone to use. Have the learners read the Gospel story on their own in whatever Bible version they have. As they read the story for themselves, have them write down anything they may have questions about or something about the story that confuses them. Encourage them to also jot down the basics of the story: the who, what, when, where, why, and how of the story. Encourage the youth to write down any questions they like, reminding them that there is no such thing as a bad question.

After everyone has had a chance to spend some time on this part of the process, place the youth in triads and have them share their reactions with each other. When the sharing is done, you may have the youth yell out their discoveries, popcorn style, as you write them down. You may want to address some of their reactions at a later time.

## Connecting to the Story (15–20 minutes)
OPTION A
*Needed: large roll of white paper, tempera paint, brushes, Bibles*
Divide participants into pairs or triads, with each group having access to Bibles, paint, brushes, and paper. Explain to the groups that they have a couple of options for this part of the process, but that all the options involve the use of paint. The groups are going to recreate the resurrection story for today by (a) creating a mural that tells the story or (b) creating and painting a worship banner based upon the story.

After they have finished their artistic retelling of the story, have the groups share their creative undertakings with the larger group.

OPTION B
*Needed: "Witness" handouts, writing utensils, Bibles, newsprint and markers*
For this part of the learning process, distribute the handout, Bibles, and writing utensils. Explain to the youth that each of them is a news reporter for the *Jerusalem News and World Report*.

Their job is to come up with questions to ask each of the three witnesses mentioned in the story as well as Jesus. There is room under each name on the handout to write down these questions. Give everyone enough time to come up with their questions, allowing them to use their Bibles if they want to refer back to the story.

After everyone has finished with their questions on the handout, divide into groups of four or whatever configuration best suits your group. Explain to the youth that they will now have to use their imagination as everyone within the group will role-play a particular character: Mary, Peter, the "other disciple," and Jesus. Once everyone has been given a character to role-play, begin your interviewing of the story characters in a round-robin manner. For example, if the character to be interviewed is Jesus, have the first reporter ask Jesus a question to respond to, then the second reporter would ask a question, and so on. After everyone has had a chance to ask a question of that character, you would then rotate to the next person and repeat the process until everyone has had a chance to be interviewed as well as interview.

When all the groups are done, bring them back into a larger grouping and have groups share some of the questions and responses they came up with for the different characters within the story. Record them on newsprint and save it for a future time, especially if some of the questions asked are especially insightful or unique.

## Exploring the Story
## (15–20 minutes)
OPTION A
*Needed: "The Story of the Resurrection" handouts, writing utensils, Bibles, commentaries on the Gospels or a good youth study Bible (optional)*
Give a copy of "The Story of the Resurrection" handouts and a writing utensil to everyone. Divide the class into groups of four or so, making sure everyone has a Bible. Within each of the groups, have the youth assign themselves one of the resurrection stories, reading their story out loud to the small group. Begin with today's story from John. After John's Gospel account has been read, use the handout to help the youth explore the four accounts.

When the groups have completed their handouts, invite the youth back into the larger group to share what they found. After the young people have shared, ask if anything new was learned about the resurrection story. Ask:
■ Do the differences between the stories change how you interpret the story?
■ Do the differences change your perception of the story?
For this step, it might be helpful for you to have done some of the research suggested in endnote 2 on the theories of the original intended audiences for the different Gospels.

OPTION B
*Needed: newsprint and marker, Bibles, Bible study resources, paper, writing utensils*
This option will help the learners explore characters within the story

that often are overlooked. Break the youth into groups and give them paper, writing utensils, pens, and Bible study helps. On posted newsprint, write the verse references for the four Gospel accounts of the resurrection: John 20:1-18, Matthew 28:1-10, Mark 16:1-8, and Luke 24:1-12. Have the groups explore these four stories and make a list of characters found in each story. After they have done so, instruct the youth to use their Bible study helps to put together a brief profile of these people. Encourage the youth to share with one another as they do their research.

When they have completed their task, bring them together into one large group again and have them share their profiles. Make note of similarities and differences among the profiles and ask clarifying questions if appropriate. Ask:

■ Do you experience the story differently through these other eyes?
■ Is there any one character you connect more to after hearing his or her profile?
■ How do these characters have an impact upon your understanding of the story?

**Living the Story
(5–10 minutes)**
OPTION A
*Needed: praise song, guitar or keyboard accompanist*
Gather everyone into a circle and spend a few moments reviewing what *you* have learned from *them* during this session. Then ask the youth if they learned something new from today's session. Do they feel differently about the resurrection

story now than they felt before this session? Remind them that this story is central to the Christian faith. It is what sets us apart from other religions. Does this story have significance to them? Can they tell you how? Consider how this story has impact upon you and share that with the young people.

Give affirmation to all of your young people for the wonderful work they have done. If you did the option with artwork, make sure it has been put on display somewhere in the room or where the congregation may view it. In closing, sing a favorite song of the group that might express the impact the resurrection has upon their faith journey.

OPTION B
*Needed: candle, matches or lighter, worship CD or tape, CD player, a container big enough for burning paper, writing utensils, paper*
As a way of closing your time, bring the young people together in a circle with a lit candle in the middle of the group. Have a worship tape or CD playing quietly in the background. Thank the group for their outstanding work this session. Reflect back to them new insights or learnings you picked up from them.

Though the resurrection is the crux of our faith as Christians, it is an event that is filled with mystery, awe, and doubt. Acknowledge these things to your youth in an open and honest manner. We all have moments like that of the man who came to Jesus shouting, "I believe; help my unbelief!" (Mark 9:24).

Pass out paper and a writing utensil to each youth and encourage them to write a prayer to God. It can be about anything. It may be praise for the power of the resurrection. It may express a doubt or fear they have about their life and faith. Whatever it is, have them take a moment to write it down.

Finally, as a way to lift their prayer up to God, have them fold their paper in half and set it on fire from the candle. Place the "prayer" in the container as the smoke billows up toward the heavens. When all have finished "praying," close your time together with an "Amen!"

## Things to Ponder

Take time after the session is over to reflect on your time with your youth. What discoveries were made that seemed to be significant to the young people? Do you sense a particular youth might need some individual follow-up? You also may want to review some of the posted questions, answers, etc., from the different options that may be helpful in the future. Thank God in your prayers for the young people who have been brought into your life.

## Looking Ahead

You may need to gather some advertisements as described in the next session. Be sure to read the session far enough in advance to give yourself time to prepare.

## Notes

1. Prizes might include gift certificates for a snack from a fast food restaurant or large candy bars or a great toy from a dollar store. They need not be expensive, but they should be things the youth would actually enjoy.
2. You may want to do some research on the four Gospels, their original audiences (as theorized by commentators), and how the audiences might contribute to the differences in their resurrection accounts. You might particularly want to be prepared for questions about the ending of the Gospel of Mark, as it is especially jarring when compared with the others. A good resource for this would be the Gospel volumes in *The New Interpreter's Bible Commentary* series (Abingdon). Or alternatively, assist the youth in doing their own exploration with the help of Bible study aids.
3. If you are using a youth study Bible, make sure it has an introduction to each Gospel that explains some of the theories about timing and audiences.

# Witness

**Mary Magdalene:**

**Peter:**

**"The other disciple":**

**Jesus:**

# The Story of the Resurrection

**John 20:1-18**

Characters:

Story details:

**Matthew 28:1-10**

Characters:

Similarities of story:

Differences:

**Mark 16:1-8**

Characters:

Similarities of story:

Differences:

**Luke 24:1-12**

Characters:

Similarities of story:

Differences:

# 4. New Heaven and New Earth

*Bible Story: Revelation 21:1-7*

Carol S. Adams

## A Story behind the Story

When God created the heavens and the earth, it was good. God said so. Earth was a paradise. There were animals of every kind. There was a garden full of luscious plants watered by a flowing river. The sun shone, the moon lit up the night sky, the gentle rains fell. People were content. It was perfect.

But then sin entered into the world, and the earth has never been the same. Think of our world today. Sure, plants and animals still live, rain still falls, the sun still shines. Yet hunger, hatred, and strife plague the planet. Grief and death, sorrow and pain are all known. People have disobeyed God and now must face the consequences. Since the beginning of sin, which is a separation from God, creation has longed for a reunion with its Maker. Wouldn't it be great to have a new earth with no more pain and no more tears?

The Old Testament prophets told of such a time (Isaiah 65:17; 66:22). Scripture also reminds us that when this new heaven and earth are established, the old will pass away and will no longer be remembered (Psalm 102:25-26; Matthew 24:35). The writer of Hebrews states it well:

> In the beginning, O Lord, you laid the foundations of the earth,
>     and the heavens are the work of your hands.
> They will perish, but you will remain. (Hebrews 1:10-11, NIV)

These Scriptures remind us that the earth is not our foundation; God is. The earth will pass away, but the promises of God remain faithful to the end.

The promise is that all believers will be united with God forever. Until that time, our earth will still have sin, our lives will still have sin. Can we bring a taste of heaven to earth now? How can we make God our foundation?

We may not be alive when the earth as we know it passes away. Sometimes it seems like the earth today is further away from God than ever. Yet the Scripture brings hope. God's promises remain faithful. The Bible begins with rebellion and ends with a reunion—a marriage between people and God.

## Enter the Story

If you're a morning person, try reading this Scripture at sunrise, when the world feels like a "new heaven and a new earth." If not, however, be sure to create a sacred space for your reading, perhaps by lighting a candle or listening to your preferred Christian music. Take a few moments to consider times when you sometimes feel separated from God: How does that feel? When does it happen? How long does that feeling last? What makes the feeling go away? After reading Revelation 21:1-7, consider those same times of separation again. How do these promises make you feel now? Pray for God's insights as you spend time with God's Word.

## Setting the Stage
## (5–10 minutes)
OPTION A
*Needed: advertisements (some featuring "new and improved" items), poster board, glue, scissors, prize or candy (optional)*
As students enter, have several advertisements around the room. Instruct students to find as many ads as possible that show a "new" or "improved" product. When a "new" or "improved" ad is found, have them cut it out and glue it to the poster board at the front of the room. Encourage them to find as many as possible. You may wish to offer a prize to the person who finds the most ads.

When all the ads are exhausted, focus everyone's attention upon the poster board. Point out several of the ads. Encourage the learners who found each ad to tell a little about it. Be sure to point out ones that seem odd or perhaps even contradict themselves.

Discuss with the learners what it means for something to be "new" or "improved."
■ Are there any standards?
■ Are the items completely new or just improved? What is the difference?
■ Is it easy to tell the difference between an old item and a "new" or "improved" item?
■ How can we tell what is a sales gimmick and what is truly improved?
■ Has anyone's life ever really been improved as a result of a "new" or "improved" product?

OPTION B
*Needed: "Neighborhood News" handouts, writing utensils, markers, CD or other music, CD player*
As youth arrive, have music playing. Give each learner a copy of the "Neighborhood News" handout. Have them develop the front page of a neighborhood newsletter. They may choose their own neighborhood, the neighborhood surrounding their school, or the neighborhood surrounding your church building. If you wish learners to work in partners, have the pairs choose one neighborhood upon which to focus.

The newsletter should give a flavor of what the neighborhood is like. It may discuss recent or upcoming events. Perhaps it will profile some people in the neighborhood or some recent landscape changes. Encourage the youth to be creative while maintaining a realistic view of what the neighborhood is really like.

Allow time for volunteers to highlight parts of their newsletters for the entire group. Affirm learners for their efforts and their willingness to share.

## Telling the Story
## (5–10 minutes) ✓ *Images, meaning*
OPTION A
*Needed: paper, markers or crayons, Bibles*
Invite the students to sit in a circle and close their eyes as you read them the Bible story. Encourage them to visualize the story as it is read.

After the first reading, give each student a piece of paper and some

## POSSIBLE YOUTH CONTACT POINTS
■ **How is God living in my neighborhood?**
■ **Will I inherit anything from God?**
■ **What will it be like to be united with God?**

## YOU MAY NEED
■ advertisements
■ newsprint or poster board
■ glue
■ scissors
■ small prize or candy (optional)
■ "Neighborhood News" handouts
■ writing utensils
■ markers or crayons
■ CD or other music
■ CD player
■ paper
■ Bibles
■ *The Message* or other contemporary paraphrase
■ "IQ Test" handouts
■ Bible study resources, such as concordances, Bible dictionaries, commentaries, and Bible encyclopedias
■ dictionary (nonbiblical)
■ scrap paper (optional)
■ index cards
■ candle
■ matches or lighter

markers or crayons. Tell them that this time, as you read the passage, they are to draw what passes through their minds as they hear the Scripture. Slowly read the passage a couple of times, allowing the learners time to draw whatever they wish in response to what they hear. If any one learner is embarrassed by his or her poor drawing skills, give this one encouragement: Remind the youth that this exercise is not about producing a masterpiece but about expressing and responding to the ideas of the story through drawing. Students may wish to draw one picture containing everything, or they may wish to draw their images in a sequence of frames, cartoon-style.

After all have added the final touches, have each person share his or her artistic expression with the group. Affirm each learner for her or his efforts. Comment on the wide variety of artistic responses.

OPTION B
*Needed:* The Message *or another contemporary paraphrase Bible,* Bibles
Gather the group and invite them to listen as you read the story. Read the passage from *The Message* paraphrase. Read it as expressively as possible. If you can get hold of several copies of *The Message* or another contemporary paraphrase, make them available to the youth.

Instruct the youth to find a partner or a group with whom to work. Each group will develop a rap or a song based on the passage from the contemporary paraphrase you are using. Encourage them to be as creative as possible. It is not neces-

sary that the song or rap follow the passage word for word. The goal is to include the main ideas of the passage. Encourage them to have a beat and even use objects in the room as rhythm instruments. Also encourage them to come up with an appropriate title for their song.

After they have prepared their songs, allow each group to present its creation. When all have shared, invite them to turn to Revelation 21:1-7 in their own Bibles. Read it through together. If learners have different translations, invite several to read from their translations. Discuss how their creative expressions were similar to or different from the real passage. Some songs or raps may have been easier to understand than others. This may be true of some of the written translations as well.

## Reacting to the Story (15–20 minutes)
OPTION A
*Needed: "IQ Test" handouts, writing utensils, Bibles*
Give each participant a copy of the "IQ Test" handout. If you used this handout during previous lessons, simply review the procedure and let them begin. If this is the first time using this handout, explain that this is an easy way to begin studying the Bible. This format is helpful in responding to the passages they read.

Read each section of the handout. Tell the youth that they can use this technique for any passage they read. The handout suggests reading the passage three times. Your group just finished reading or hearing it at least twice. Suggest they silently review it at least one more time on their own.

Give them time to write down a few things for each section. Ask volunteers to share insights. It will be fun to see the variety of responses! Be sure to affirm their differing responses. Then ask volunteers to share their questions. Encourage them by suggesting that perhaps some of these questions will get answered before the end of the session. You may even wish to record the questions on newsprint to refer to later.

OPTION B

*Needed: paper, markers, newsprint or poster board*

Divide the youth into small groups. Have paper, markers, and poster board or newsprint available.

Instruct each group that they are to develop a brochure or commercial for the New Heaven and New Earth. Each group will have an opportunity to share their presentation. Encourage each group to create pictures to use either in the brochure or the commercial presentation.

Encourage the groups to think about how they could make the New Heaven and Earth appealing—to "sell" it. Have them look at the passage for ideas on what the place would be like. Encourage them to think of the benefits to those listening. Why would they care about the New Heaven and Earth? Why would they want to go there? How is this New Heaven and Earth different from where they are now?

After everyone has had time to prepare, give each group time to present their brochure or com-

mercial. Be sure to affirm each group for their creativity and content.

## Connecting to the Story (15–20 minutes)

OPTION A

*Needed: newsprint and marker, Bibles*

Ask the youth if any of them ever think about their wedding day. Ask them to share some of the things they dream about for that special day. If they haven't spent time thinking about it yet, ask them about weddings they have been involved in—perhaps those of siblings, relatives, or family friends. What have they noticed about the preparations for that day? What is involved in planning a wedding?

On the newsprint, make a list as the youth share. When you have gathered several ideas, review the list. How many of the thoughts have to do with how the participants will look on that day? Perhaps the girls will mention their dress or their hair or how they walk down the aisle. Boys might mention renting tuxes or making other preparations.

You might want to research, ahead of time, other cultural traditions about weddings, particularly those of ancient Palestine. Share these findings with the youth, if you have them.

Turn to the Revelation 21 passage again. Have a volunteer read verse 2 out loud. Have the group discuss what this verse might mean.

- Why would a city be like a bride?
- Why would the writer choose that image?
- Are there any other examples of bride imagery in the Bible?

- Have you ever heard the idea that Christians are the bride of Christ? Where does that idea come from? What do you think about it?

OPTION B
*Needed:* **The Message** *or another contemporary paraphrase*
Have a volunteer read Revelation 21:1-7 from a contemporary paraphrase. Perhaps you will want to have the student read it twice so the listeners get the full impact.

The paraphrase known as *The Message* includes the line "Look! Look! God has moved into the neighborhood, making his home with men and women!" Get your youth's ideas on what that might mean. After some sharing, prompt further discussion using questions such as the following:
- Is God moving into our neighborhoods, or are we moving into God's? Does it make a difference?
- How would your neighborhood be different if Jesus were living in one of the residences?
- Think more about your own neighborhood. Is God living there? How do you see or not see God living there?
- When God comes to live somewhere, it is a "new" place. How can you make your neighborhood a "new neighborhood" for God?
- What specific things can you do this week to make it a reality?

**Exploring the Story
(15–20 minutes)**
OPTION A
*Needed: newsprint and marker, Bibles, concordance*
In this Revelation account, we see a new heaven and a new earth.

Review some of the images that are painted in the passage. List some of these characteristics (such as no more tears or death) on a sheet of newsprint.

What other images of heaven or paradise do we find in the Bible? Ask learners to look up other passages that have to do with heaven or paradise. Encourage them to use a concordance to find other places in the Bible where those words are used. As learners find passages, have them read them aloud to the group. Add to the list any new characteristics mentioned. You may also wish to make a list of the passages in which these characteristics were found.

Here are a few passages to help get the group started:
- Genesis 1–2
- 2 Corinthians 12:1-4
- Philippians 3:20-21
- Revelation 12:7

OPTION B
*Needed: Bibles, dictionary, Bible dictionary or concordance, scrap paper, writing utensils*
Have everyone open their Bibles to Revelation 21. Draw their attention to verse 7. Invite a volunteer to read that verse aloud. Ask for feedback on what that verse means. Get several responses. Encourage the group to interact with each other's responses.

After several have shared, challenge them to examine the word "inherit." First, have the youth attempt to write a definition of *inherit* on scrap paper or the back of a handout (if you've used one previously). Next, invite them to look in the dictionary and Bible dictionary to come up with a thorough definition. Invite others to look in a concordance to find other verses that speak of inheritance. Have them use those verses to bring insight as well. Prompt them to think about how something is inherited. Must someone die in order for there to be an inheritance? Also, have them pinpoint what is being inherited.

Invite the youth to consider the following:

■ How do these new insights affect our interpretation of Revelation 21:7?

■ What about the part that says that those who overcome or conquer will inherit? To what is that referring?

After the discussion, invite the youth to revisit the definition they wrote earlier in the step and now rewrite the definition to include everything they've discovered during their study. In terms of this verse, what does the word *inherit* mean?

## Living the Story (5–10 minutes)

OPTION A

*Needed: index cards, writing utensils, candle, matches or lighter*

Gather the group together and instruct them to sit on the floor in a circle. Place the candle in the center and light it. Invite the group to reflect back over the lesson. Review the key discussion points of the lesson: a new heaven and earth versus the old ones; a bride being prepared for her husband; God dwelling in our neighborhoods; what is involved in inheriting; and what things we are inheriting.

Tell the group that now has come the time of commitment for each one of them. Pass out index cards and writing utensils. Ask them to write down one or two things they will commit to as a result of studying this lesson. Some possible commitments might include the following:

■ I will make my neighborhood a "new" neighborhood for God.

■ I will be an heir to God.

■ I will prepare myself for God as a bride prepares for her husband.

Encourage the youth to take general commitments (such as the ones listed) and come up with at least one specific way to live it out. After all have written their commitments, close in a prayer. Invite learners to pray silently or out loud, asking for God's help in carrying out their commitments.

OPTION B

*Needed: newsprint and markers*

As a group, brainstorm ways that you could make your youth group a "new heaven on earth." Talk about a few key areas, such as these:

■ How can we prepare each youth group member for God's presence?

■ How can we help each other grow closer to God?

■ How can we make our youth group a "neighborhood" where God's presence is vividly seen?

■ How can we make it a place where God can comfort our tears and pain and where God can use us to comfort others?

■ How can we show visitors and friends that our youth group is a place that is different from the rest of the world?

List your ideas on newsprint. Commit as a group to making your group a "new heaven on earth." Pray over your commitments. Hang the newsprint in a place where all will be reminded of the commitments made.

## Things to Ponder

How did this session go over? How did the group respond to the idea of God dwelling in their neighborhoods? How might you encourage them to make their neighborhoods a place where others notice God? As always, pray for your group this week.

## Looking Ahead

If you are planning on painting a wall mural as part of Option A of "Living the Story" in Session 7, you will need to begin finalizing your plans for location, supplies, and schedule. Consider bringing in an adult artist as an adviser, if you have one in the congregation, but make sure the youth artists are the true designers and creators of the mural. Additionally, for the next session, you may need to gather some praise and worship music and some Christian music videos. Your local Christian bookstore will have these, and you may be able to find them online as well.

# Neighborhood News

# IQ Test

*An easy way to begin studying a Scripture passage is to give it the IQ Test.*

Begin by reading the passage three times. (It helps to read it out loud at least one of those times.)

## Insights

Record any insights you have about the passage. An insight may be simple observations about the passage: who is writing, where the story takes place, etc. It may also be anything that particularly stands out to you.

## Questions

Write down any questions you have about the passage. The questions may be about the story line, any new words you encountered, or even how the passage applies to your life today.

# 5. Psalm of Praise

*Bible Story: Psalm 150*

Karen Yee

## A Story behind the Story

The Book of Psalms is a collection of prayers, songs, and liturgies written to celebrate or remember different holidays and rituals. It is also a collection of various authors' expressions of their personal feelings and experiences. Times of joy, sorrow, confusion, fear, thanksgiving—the whole range of human emotions and experiences is beautifully expressed in the various psalms.

The collection of the Psalms most likely took place over a long period of time in Israel's life as a community of faith. The emotions expressed here are those of generations of the faithful. They are equally apt for the faithful of today. Perhaps our best lesson in prayer is that which comes from praying the Psalms. Grappling with the deepest and most base emotions expressed in them (such as in Psalm 58), as well as allowing our souls to exult (Psalm 98), will allow us to develop in our faith journey and to see how our relationship with God permeates everything we do. If we allow ourselves the time to read each and every one of the Psalms, we will come across words and phrases that may take us aback. We like to think of the Psalms as beautiful poetry, but sometimes they are harsh in their depiction of human life. They contain the beauty and the beast, as it were, both of which we need to deal with in our attempts to be God's people.

Psalm 150 is the final hymn in the collection. Taken by itself, out of context, we might appreciate it as a nice little verse of praise, suitable for using as a call to worship or a quick prayer. However, if we've read straight through from Psalm 1 to this point, an infinitely more fulfilling image emerges. Even after the sorrow, even after we've spent hours bashing heaven with our complaints, we can still praise God. When the lights are down and we're alone with our God, we can exult in God's greatness. As we reflect on our lives, which are filled with loneliness, loss, and insecurity, we can celebrate God's mighty deeds. Having laid our troubles at God's feet, with no assurance of how God's answer will play out in the reality of our lives, we can declare, "Let everything that breathes praise the Lord!"

## Enter the Story

Find a quiet spot and prepare your heart to listen to God. Pray before you begin reading, asking God to illuminate some truth that may apply to you personally or to the youth. This psalm may be very familiar, but read expectantly. Expect to encounter and worship God in a fresh way. Read meditatively and reflect on things that catch your attention and interest.

Have paper and a pen nearby. Read through the psalm at least three times in this way. It is an invitation to come praise. Who is invited? Where is the celebration? How shall we celebrate? Why do we praise? Reflect on a time in your own life when praise overflowed as it does in this psalm. Pray that God will allow you to experience true praise in your heart so that you may be able to lead your youth to praise as well.

## POSSIBLE YOUTH CONTACT POINTS

- **What is the difference between praise and worship?**
- **How do I experience and express praise in my life?**
- **Why doesn't church feel like praise to God?**
- **How can I praise God when my life is going badly?**

## YOU MAY NEED

- **Bibles**
- **writing utensils**
- **paper**
- **hymnbooks**
- **different musical instruments**
- **ordinary objects, such as combs, rocks, cups, sticks, tubs, paper plates, beads, metal tools, rubber bands, string**
- **craft supplies, including tape, scissors, glue, paper**
- **various Bible translations, such as** NRSV, NIV, KJV, NLT, TLB, *The Message*
- **praise and worship songbooks**
- **praise and worship CDs**
- **Christian music videos**
- **"Create Your Own Psalm of Praise" handouts**
- **Bible study resources, including commentaries on Psalms, Bible dictionaries, concordances, encyclopedias, etc.**
- **study Bibles**
- **newsprint or chalkboard prepared with list of questions from Option A of "Exploring the Story"**
- **"Psalms of Praise" handouts**

## Setting the Stage (5–10 minutes)

OPTION A

*Needed: paper, writing utensils, hymnals (optional)*

Divide the youth into at least three groups. Give each group a piece of paper and writing utensil and ask the groups to brainstorm a list of all the praise songs they know. After three minutes, call time and collect the writing utensils. Tell the class they're going to play "Praise Song Elimination." When you point to a group, everyone in the group must begin to sing one of the songs on their list. They must continue to sing until you point to another group. No group is allowed to repeat a song that has already been sung. If a group repeats a song or does not respond with a song in a timely manner, that group is eliminated. The winning team is the group that has the last song.

After you've played the game, spend some time together talking about what function praise songs have in worship. Why are they called "praise songs"? Are there any elements that are common to all praise songs? (If your youth do not sing praise songs as a part of their tradition, have them brainstorm hymns of praise. Afterward, check in a hymnal to find more examples.)

OPTION B

*Needed: different musical instruments, odd objects (e.g., combs, rocks, cups, sticks, tubs, paper plates, beads, metal tools), craft supplies (e.g., rubber bands, string, tape, scissors)*

Prior to the session, collect all the different kinds of musical instru-

ments you can find. They can be real, but even toy instruments will work. You might be able to find jaw harps, nose flutes, or tin whistles at dollar stores, and if so, you can give these to the youth to take home at the end of the session.

You will also need to gather together different objects and craft supplies that the youth can use to create their own instruments. When the youth arrive, give them an opportunity to experiment with the different instruments and to create new ones with the different objects provided. As the youth are experimenting, ask if any of them play instruments. If so, which ones? Where do they play (school band, jazz band, garage band, etc.)? How does playing their instrument make them feel? Have they ever played their instrument in church? When? How did that make them feel?

## Telling the Story (5–10 minutes)

OPTION A

*Needed: a variety of Bible translations and versions of Psalm 150, different instruments (optional)*

Psalm 150 invites and instructs us to praise the Lord in different places and in various ways. Before the reading, ask the youth where they usually praise God. Do they praise God in church? Do they praise God at home? What about at school?

Let the class know that they are going to have a chance now to put their praise into action, using today's psalm. Make sure the youth have a selection of Bible versions among them, and instruct everyone to turn to Psalm 150. If there are musical instruments or created ones available from the previous step, have some of the youth take their favorite ones with them. Take a praise walk around the building and outside the church facilities, and at different locations, ask individuals to read from the different versions of Psalm 150. During each reading, encourage youth who have instruments to play them for a moment directly following the reading. (Be sure that you are not disturbing other classes!) When you've returned to the classroom space, have everyone return the instruments, be seated, and read Psalm 150 one last time in the version of your choice.

OPTION B

*(If you chose Option B under "Setting the Stage," you may want to use the following exercise for this segment.)*
*Needed: different musical instruments, any new "musical instruments" that were created, Bibles*

After a period of experimenting with the musical instruments and their new "musical instruments," ask the youth to prepare for the reading of Psalm 150. As a group, or using different individuals, read Psalm 150. As the youth read, use the instruments to make a joyful noise together. Read through the psalm several times, each time experimenting with a different combination of instruments and volume. Have the youth find matches for the various instruments and expressions mentioned in the verses: What instrument would produce a trumpetlike sound? A lute or harp sound? Cymbals? Have the youth develop a short praise dance and

then decide how they want to praise at the last verse—maybe a cheer or clapping or shouting the words.

### Reacting to the Story (15–20 minutes)
OPTION A
*Needed: Bibles, hymnbooks, songbooks, praise and worship CDs*
Inform the youth that the Book of Psalms is an anthology of songs, poems, and prayers that were sung, spoken, and prayed by individuals and communities in a variety of settings. Let them know that these psalms developed over generations, just like the hymns in traditional church hymnbooks. If your congregation sings only contemporary praise songs, have the youth consider whether these songs will still be sung by their grandchildren or great-grandchildren. In one way, Psalms could be viewed as the hymnbook or songbook for God's people.

Ask the youth to react to Psalm 150.
■ What did you like or dislike about the psalm?
■ What insights does it give you about how the early believers worshipped?
■ How is it similar to the way we worship?
In response to that last question, ask the youth to compare Psalm 150 with some of their own songs of praise or hymns. Allow the youth some time to look through the different praise and worship books, CDs, and hymnbooks, and ask them to find songs that are similar to Psalm 150. How are they similar and how are they different? If you've got time, sing one or two of the selections or listen to them on CD. Compare the

lyrics side by side with Psalm 150. How are they similar? Different?

OPTION B
*Needed: Bibles*
Psalms often express deep feelings and emotions, and they can also stir up similar feelings. After listening to Psalm 150, invite the youth to share some "popcorn" responses to the questions you will be asking. Ask them to say the first thought or image that comes to their mind.
■ What color comes to mind?
■ What action do you want to do?
■ What feeling arises for you?
■ What song or phrase comes to mind?
■ How does it influence how you think or respond to God?

See if the youth can imagine the person who wrote this psalm. What might have been happening in that person's life? Encourage the youth to be as imaginative as possible: When do they most feel like praising God? When might the psalm writer have felt like praising God?

**Connecting to the Story
(15–20 minutes)**
OPTION A
*Needed: variety of songbooks, including hymnals and praise and worship books, CDs, Bibles, Christian music videos, Christian writings, paper, writing utensils*
Give the youth freedom to stray completely from their normal style or liturgy, and invite them to create a praise service of their own. Depending on the size of the group, create groups of no more than six people. (This way everyone will have the opportunity to give input.) Allow time for the youth to share what they planned. As the youth cre-

ate their praise services, have them consider these different elements:
■ Describe the setting of the service (location, time).
■ What kind of atmosphere (lighting, decoration, sounds) do you want to have?
■ How would you begin the service—call to worship, prayer, song, video, music, activity?
■ What is the focus of your praise service (God's power, faithfulness, love, lordship, creation, forgiveness)?
■ What song or hymns will you include?
■ What Scriptures or reading will you include?
■ How do you want to close the service?

Once they've developed their worship plans, consider how they might go about actually using these plans. Could they go to the pastor or church council to schedule a special worship celebration? Could they use them at a youth retreat or regional youth event, or could they schedule them for the beginning of the next several youth meetings?

OPTION B
*Needed: "Create Your Own Psalm of Praise" handouts, writing utensils*
Remind the youth that many of the psalms were written by ordinary individuals as their way of expressing their love or feelings to God, but they are not the only places where praises to God can be found. In Luke's advent story, he includes Mary's song of praise in response to the news that she has been chosen to be the mother of God's own son. Read Luke 1:45-55. In her song of praise, Mary thanks God and rejoices in God's faithfulness. Using the "Create Your Own

Psalm of Praise" handout and Mary's song of praise as a guide, invite the youth to create their own psalms. Give the youth the freedom to use the form provided or to create a psalm of praise using any style they are comfortable with. Affirm that their personal experiences and cultural influences only add to the beauty of praise.

**Exploring the Story
(15–20 minutes)**
OPTION A
*Needed: Bibles, Bible commentaries on Psalms, study Bibles, newsprint or chalkboard prepared with the list of questions below*
As one reads through the entire Book of Psalms, it is easy to see its variety. This collection includes psalms of lament from an individual and from a community, thanksgiving psalms of an individual and of a community, hymns or songs of praise, royal psalms, wisdom psalms, entrance liturgies, prophetic exhortations, psalms of confidence and trust, as well some that are a mix of the above. Invite the youth to use a variety of Bible study helps to begin exploring the different varieties.

Divide the youth into different groups and assign each group one or two of the different kinds of psalms to research. Consider writing these questions on newsprint or a chalkboard ahead of time to help guide the groups' research:
■ What are some of the characteristics of a particular kind of psalm?
■ What makes it unique?
■ How often does this kind of psalm appear?
■ What does the psalm say about God?

■ What is the response from the people?
Instruct the groups to each select a psalm to share that is typical of the particular kind of psalm they are studying. At the end of the time, allow each group to share their findings.

OPTION B
*Needed: Bibles, Bible commentaries, books on the Psalms, study Bible resources, "Psalms of Praise" handouts, pencils*
Psalm 150 is just one of many songs of praise found in the Book of Psalms. Using the handout called "Psalms of Praise," allow the youth to select a different praise psalm to explore in closer detail. Once they've done so, have them break into pairs to share their findings—try to make sure the pairs include two different psalms. Once they've done so, give the youth some of the information about the different types of psalms from "A Story behind the Story." Invite the youth to look at different psalms at random and see if they can figure out what kind each psalm is (see Option A above for a concise list of types). Ask: *What type of Psalm would you feel most like praying right now if you were alone with God?* (They need not answer aloud.) Invite them to find a psalm that feels meaningful to them at this moment and write down the psalm number so that they can spend some more time with it at home.

**Living the Story
(5–10 minutes)**
OPTION A
*(If you chose Option B in "Telling the Story," you may want to use this option.)*

*Needed: "Create Your Own Psalm of Praise" handouts (completed), musical instruments (optional)*

Take a few moments to review the session. See if the youth can name (without prompting) some different types of psalms or the elements that make up a psalm of praise. Invite them to mention some hymns or praise songs they discussed earlier or other highlights of the session. Ask if anyone had a favorite psalm that he or she read at any time during the session. What makes it a favorite? Invite the students to share their psalms of praise, written on the first handout, as a closing prayer of thanksgiving and praise. If they would like, they may use an instrument to go along with their psalm.

OPTION B

*(If you chose Option A under "Connecting to the Story," you may want to use the following exercise for this segment.)*
*Needed: notes from planning a service of praise, music, songbooks, CDs, prayers*

Remind the youth that the invitation is to anyone, anytime, anyplace, and using anything to "come, praise the Lord!" Take a few moments as a class to choose different segments from the worship services planned during Option A of "Connecting the Story" and combine them into one brief service of praise. Each group should lead the rest of the class in their own portion of the service. Obviously, you will want to choose one segment of each group's work. After you've had your worship service together, close in prayer.

Finally, encourage the youth to follow through on any plans they made to share their worship services with the congregation as a whole. Make sure assignments are understood, and follow up with the youth during the week to plan the service itself. An alternative would be to schedule a time when your group may attend a worship service from a different tradition or culture. If your church shares a building with another church, see if you could attend the worship of that other church. Get names from the local ecumenical council of other congregations, synagogues, or mosques you could attend. If you are able to do so, be sure to spend some time with your group discussing the experience afterward. What were the similarities? The differences? How was praise expressed during the worship you visited? Were the psalms used? How?

## Things to Ponder

Expressions of praise in the Bible vary, and this is also true in our modern-day church settings. The style of praise is often influenced by culture, environment, liturgy, and generational differences. It is important that the youth are not too quick to judge the quality or sincerity of others' praise if it appears different from the way they experience or express praise.

## Looking Ahead

For the next option, you may need to gather some props for one of the activities. You may also want to consider what snacks you would like to provide.

~~~~~~

# Create Your Own Psalm of Praise

_____'s Song of Praise (Add your name)

And  _____ said, (Add your name)

My soul magnifies the Lord, and my spirit rejoices in God my Savior, for God has looked with favor on the lowliness of God's servant. Surely, from now on all generations will call me blessed; for the Mighty One has done great things for me, and holy is God's name.

God's mercy is . . .

God has shown strength . . .

God has . . .

Let everything that breathes praise the Lord!
Praise the Lord!

# Psalms of Praise

*Choose one of the following psalms of praise to explore:*

**Psalm 100**   **Psalm 103**   **Psalm 113**   **Psalm 135**
**Psalm 146**   **Psalm 147**   **Psalm 148**   **Psalm 149**

*Use the following questions to assist your exploration.*

**According to Psalm _____**

**1.** Who should praise?

**2.** Why should we praise?

**3.** How should we praise?

**4.** What characteristics of God are exalted?

**5.** What special images or figurative language are used?

**6.** What verse or verses were disturbing or confused you?

**7.** Select a verse (or verses) from the psalm that captured your attention or touched your heart. Write it out below.

# 6. Lord, Teach Us to Pray

*Bible Story: Luke 10:38–11:10*

Paul Mast Hewitt

### A Story behind the Story

This passage has been extended to cover three different stories: the account of Jesus' visit to Mary and Martha's house, Luke's version of Jesus teaching the disciples the Lord's Prayer, and the parable of the persistent neighbor. In many ways, these three stories are distinct from one another and deserve to be dealt with separately. For this reason, in this session many of the options allow the learners to choose which section of the passage to study.

The writer of Luke's Gospel weaves many themes throughout the book. First, commentators have noted Luke's attention to women. He mentions the women supporters of Jesus' ministry a number of times, starting with Luke's unique treatment of Mary in the birth account and including the account of Jesus' visit to Mary and Martha's house, which is mentioned in none of the other Gospels. See Luke 8:1-3 for one significant reference to Jesus' women supporters. Second, prayer plays a special role in this Gospel. Jesus is repeatedly described as going off to pray, and he teaches about prayer in numerous places. He also mentions prayer frequently (in 1:13, for example). Third, Luke incorporates a unique section defined by Jesus' journey toward Jerusalem, which begins in 9:51. This journeying motif is important to our section as Jesus' travels necessitated his staying at the home of some of his followers and required their hospitality to support his ministry. The need for daily bread is even more profound for itinerant travelers.

Hospitality was an important unwritten law in the ancient Near East. The story of Mary and Martha, along with that of the friend who has a traveler arrive at midnight, are understood better when considered in the light of those hospitality practices. Any Bible dictionary should have an article on hospitality that would be worth reading before the lesson.

The stories contained in one Gospel are often remarkable for their parallels in one or more of the other three Gospels. Equally or even more remarkable are those stories that lack a parallel. The first section of this session's Scripture—that about Mary and Martha—is nowhere to be found in the other Gospels. That it is unique in Luke tells us something about Luke's own interests. While Luke's account of the Lord's Prayer is not unique, it is distinct from Matthew's version. These differences may give rise to great discussion in your class, so be prepared to respond to the questions and debates that may develop.

### Enter the Story

These stories are familiar to many of us and it is easy to read quickly through them without pausing to let them speak to us in a fresh way. We, in effect, become like Martha, in a hurry to get the task done, forgetting that this is God's Word for us today. Take time to read Luke 10:38–11:10 once more and sit

## POSSIBLE YOUTH CONTACT POINTS

- **Does God hear my prayers?**
- **Does God really answer prayer?**
- **Why is it so hard to sit and listen?**
- **What did Jesus say about prayer?**
- **What is prayer?**
- **Do we have to keep asking for the same thing?**

## YOU MAY NEED

- snack (unprepared) and supplies for serving
- clock or watch with a second hand
- at least three Bibles of the same version
- three prop bags (see Option A, "Telling the Story")
- three or four assistants to mime the story
- newsprint or chalkboard
- markers or chalk
- paper
- writing utensils
- Bible study resources, such as Bible dictionaries, commentaries, and concordances
- "Dig a Little Deeper" handouts
- "Consider This" handouts
- newsprint with the Lord's Prayer written out

silently for five minutes, reflecting on the stories and what God would offer you in these words. At the end of the five minutes, you might want to write down your reflections, perhaps in your own journal.

### Setting the Stage (5–10 minutes)

OPTION A

*Needed: snack and serving supplies*

To start things off this week, dramatize the story of Mary and Martha. Bring a snack, but do not completely prepare it before the lesson. As the first learners arrive, begin preparing the snack, working hurriedly. Exaggerate the sense of distraction as much as possible so the learners know something is up, but take care to keep it believable. If there is a second leader, you could have one greet the youth individually in a friendly, relaxed manner while the other frantically prepares the snack.

After everyone has arrived, share the snack with the group and talk about what they have experienced. How did they feel about being ignored while the leader was distracted by preparations for the meeting? If time allows, you could also talk about the last time they had people over for a meal or the last time they went to someone else's for a meal. Did the host greet the visitors and talk with them? Was the host busy with preparations and unable to attend to the guests? Which would feel better to a guest?

OPTION B

*Needed: clock or watch*

After greeting the youth, have the group break into pairs. You may

want to encourage them to pair with someone they don't know well, especially separating good friends and siblings. Explain that they will each have an opportunity to listen to their partners introduce themselves with basic biographical information (or some specific thing that happened in the last week, if they know each other well). Tell them that you will announce when it is time to start and stop and that afterward each will be introducing the other to the group. They will each have one minute to talk.

Tell them to begin, and after a minute, to switch. After two minutes, have them introduce their partner to the group. (If you have a larger group, you may want to have three or four pairs form subgroups and have them do the introductions in these groups to save time.) If you have time, you could talk about listening, using questions along these lines:

- How long can you listen—what's your attention span?
- Do you have a hard time listening attentively?

When all have finished, explain that you are going to look at a story in which one of the characters chose to listen.

### Telling the Story (5–10 minutes)

OPTION A

*Needed: at least three Bibles, props in three different bags for each section of the passage*

Beforehand, you may want to gather props that would be appropriate for each story in the passage (although the activity can be done without props). Suggestions for props include the following: pots, pans, broom, plates, and cups for Luke 10:38-42; biblical costumes for Luke 11:1-4; a sleeping bag and pillow for Luke 11:5-10.

In class, divide the youth into three subgroups. Explain that each group will be responsible to present part of the Scripture for the day and that they can choose to present it in any way they want. The only rule is that it must include the text as it is written (although they can add narration or other elements). They can use drama, song, sound effects, recitation, or anything else they can think of. Encourage them to be creative. Assign each group one of the following stories: Luke 10:38-42, Luke 11:1-4, Luke 11:5-10. Remind them that they must plan quickly.

Give the group five minutes or so to prepare, then have each present their respective story. After each group has done their presentation, thank them and say something positive about the presentation or their effort.

## OPTION B

*Needed: volunteers prepared to mime the story*

The week before this lesson, ask three or four people to help you mime (face paint optional) the story for this week. You will want to meet with the mimes to rehearse prior to class time. When you meet with them, read through the passage together and develop appropriate actions for each section of the story. Encourage the mimes to exaggerate facial expressions and gestures. The beginning part should be easy to develop appropriate mime for, as it is narrative and the mime can simply follow the actions of the characters. After you have choreographed the mime, practice with the mimes at least once before class time.

When it is time to read the story, invite the mimes forward, explaining to the rest of the group that you have invited a few people to help you present the story. After the presentation, thank your assistants.

## Reacting to the Story (15–20 minutes)

OPTION A

After hearing the story, ask the youth to consider all the characters that they have heard about: Mary, Martha, Jesus, the disciples, the friend who knocks on the door at midnight, the friend who is woken up at midnight. You might want to ask the group to briefly describe who each character was and what happened to them as you run through the list, to remind the youth of the different characters.

Next, explain to the youth that they are to choose one of those characters with whom they identify—one who seems to be like them or who struck a chord with them in some way. Give them a few moments to make a choice (and tell them they really do have to make a choice, even if they only partially identify with a character). Explain that you are going to call out the names of the characters in quick succession and, as you do so, the youth are to stand up when they hear the name of the character whom they chose; they are then to sit down again right away. Read the list of characters above, with only the slightest of pauses between each.

After you've done so, have the youth gather into groups based on the characters they've chosen to discuss why they chose that character. If someone is in a group by himself or herself, form a group with that person yourself for the discussion.

OPTION B
*Needed: newsprint and markers or chalkboard and chalk*
Take a moment or two to review the three stories the group just heard read or saw mimed. Invite volunteers to quickly summarize each story. (If you chose Option A above, you might want to be sure the youth have read the stories in their Bibles as well.) After the youth have reviewed the stories, ask them if anything surprised them about any of the three stories, or ask them what questions were raised by the stories. Record (or have one of the students record) their responses to these questions on the newsprint or chalkboard.

## Connecting to the Story (15–20 minutes)
OPTION A
*Needed: paper, writing utensils*
Hand out blank or lined paper, along with a writing utensil to each youth. Explain that the youth are to choose one of the three stories (Luke 10:38-42, 11:1-4, or 11:5-10) to paraphrase or modernize. You may need to explain that paraphrasing is telling the same story in your own words, while modernizing is getting the same point across by telling a present-day version of the story.

Invite the youth to use their creativity and have fun with this step.

If they choose to modernize the story, ask them to give consideration to what people, places, or things might be included in the story to relate it to their community and time period. If some youth are more inclined toward drawing than writing, they might choose to draw a cartoon-style storyboard with dialogue or a mural-style drawing depicting the scene. Again, however, they should take care to express the basic feelings, meanings, and actions they believe are represented in the story they choose.

If you have time, you could ask for volunteers to read their stories or show their artwork.

OPTION B
*Needed: paper, writing utensils*
Invite the group to consider the three stories they just heard, especially the characters who appear in these stories. If you chose Option A of "Reacting to the Story," you might invite the students to use the character they chose in that option for this next step. But regardless of which option you chose in that earlier segment, the youth may now choose any character who particularly interests them. Ask the group, "If you were [their character of choice], what would you do or say in the story?" Invite the youth to take a moment to think about the question and how their chosen character might respond, then to spend a few moments writing in their journals or on paper the story from that character's point of view.

After youth have had sufficient time for their work, invite the youth to talk about why they chose that character and share their writings as they may choose. Have as many volunteers talk about their responses as time allows.

## Exploring the Story (15–20 minutes)

OPTION A

*Needed: "Dig a Little Deeper" handouts, writing utensils, Bibles, Bible study resources*

Have the learners choose which story they would like to study in depth: Luke 10:38-42, Luke 11:1-4, or Luke 11:5-10. Separate learners into three groups depending on which story they would like to study and have them gather in different areas of the room. You may want to ask some to change if the three groups are quite unequal in size. If you have a small group, the learners could individually work on the story of their choice or the group could collectively choose one story to study. Give out copies of the "Dig a Little Deeper" handout, then explain to the youth that they can choose within their subgroup which project or theme to work on for their story. If you have large subgroups, you could ask them to have some people from their group work on each theme or project. At least one person from the group should record discoveries from the group's research and answers to the questions.

After they have had five or ten minutes to work on their projects, have one person from each subgroup report to the other groups something the group discovered from their research.

OPTION B

*Needed: "Consider This" handouts, writing utensils, construction paper (optional)*

Give each of the learners a copy of the "Consider This" handout and a writing utensil. Learners can work through this handout individually or in small groups. Have them read the quote and answer the questions with their own opinions. Groups can discuss the questions among themselves. After they have had an opportunity to work on it, ask if anybody would like to report on any insights they have had. If you have extra time, consider having some construction paper available and allowing the youth time to copy part of the quotation onto the paper, decorating it as they choose, and bringing it home to remind them of their study on prayer. You may also want to challenge them to memorize the part of the Scripture story or Bonhoeffer quotation that is most meaningful to them. If you do this, decide upon an appropriate time to have them recite their chosen memorization. Be sure to celebrate their accomplishments. (But be careful here—it should not be a competition. Memorization is merely a helpful tool to give us a mental "library" of Scripture to call upon during difficult times for the rest of our lives.)

## Living the Story (5–10 minutes)

OPTION A

*Needed: paper, writing utensils, newsprint and markers (optional)*

Give each learner paper and a writing utensil. Invite the youth to respond to the following questions on paper:

- What is one thing you learned from today's lesson?
- What is one thing you might do differently because of something you learned today?

Have them keep their papers someplace safe, where no one else could see it but where they might be able to refer to it later on as they reflect further on their learnings. An option (if your group has significant trust built up) might be to post two sheets of newsprint on the walls, each with one of the above questions written on the top of it. Have each youth choose a marker and write in his or her responses on the newsprint. They needn't sign it. The newsprint may then remain on the classroom walls throughout the remainder of the year as a reminder of this lesson. (If you choose to do this, be sure to title the newsprint with the session title.) Close with prayer.

OPTION B
*Needed: the Lord's Prayer written on newsprint*
Before the lesson, write the Lord's Prayer on newsprint large enough for the group to be able to read it easily (having it written will avoid any difficulties with people knowing different versions or with embarrassing anybody who might not know it). Place the newsprint someplace where everyone will be able to see it. Gather the group together into a circle and hold hands. Remind the youth that the disciples may have had the oppor-

tunity to ask Jesus to teach them how to do anything; what they chose was to ask Jesus to teach them how to pray. This shows us how important prayer is to our relationship with God. Just as conversation with friends is how we get to know them better, gain support, share our good times, or get advice, so conversation with God does all those same things. Bring the group's attention to the newsprint and tell them that the Lord's Prayer is Jesus' way of teaching us how to pray. Invite the group to share in it together now, remembering that you are praying words that Christians have been praying through the centuries, starting with Jesus' original disciples. Pray it together out loud; then close with your own prayer.

**Things to Ponder**
Nearly everybody knows people who have prayed for healing but have not been healed. Some of your students may have had a family member who asked but did not receive. They may bring up some of these experiences during this lesson. These students may need personal follow-up to deal with their pain individually. Even so, do not stifle their expression of frustration or pain in the class.

**Looking Ahead**
For the next session you may need a collection of artistic depictions of creation and a short story based on creation. Be sure to read through the session in enough time to gather items together.

# Dig a Little Deeper

*Choose one of the stories listed below and work through the study suggestions.*
*Use the back of this page for your notes.*

## Mary and Martha, Luke 10:38-42

*Choose one of the themes below to look at more closely.*

*Hospitality:* Hospitality was very important in Jesus' day. Look up "hospitality" in a Bible dictionary. How does this shed light on Martha's reaction to Mary?

Look up Luke 10:1-12, especially verses 3-7. How do Jesus' instructions shed light on the story of Mary and Martha?

*Women:* The role of women in ancient Israel was very different than it is in today's society. Look up "woman" in a Bible dictionary. Is there anything surprising in Jesus' treatment of Mary and Martha in light of women's roles in ancient Israel?

Use a concordance to look up other stories of women in Luke.

## The Lord's Prayer, Luke 11:1-4

*Choose one of the projects below.*

*Compare:* Compare Luke 11:1-4 with Matthew 6:9-13, going through them phrase by phrase. What is the same? What is different? Do the differences change the meaning or add meaning to the prayer? Why do you suppose they are different? How does this help you understand prayer?

*Search:* Use a concordance to find other times in Luke when Jesus talked about prayer or prayed. How do the other passages help you understand Luke 11:1-4? How do all of these passages help you understand the role of prayer in Jesus' life? How does this help you understand the role of prayer in your life?

## Midnight Friend, Luke 11:5-8

*Choose one of the projects below.*

*Hospitality:* Hospitality was very important in Jesus' day. Look up "hospitality" in a Bible dictionary. How does this shed light on the persistence of the friend who had a traveler arrive at night?

Look up Luke 10:1-12, especially verses 3-7. How do Jesus' instructions shed light on the story of the persistent friend?

*Prayer:* Use a concordance to find other times in Luke when Jesus talked about prayer or prayed. How do the other passages help you understand Luke 11:5-8? How do all of these passages help you understand the role of prayer in Jesus' life? How does this help you understand the role of prayer in your life?

# Consider This

*Dietrich Bonhoeffer wrote: "The beginning of the day should not be burdened and oppressed with . . . concerns for the day's work. At the threshold of the new day stands the Lord. . . . Therefore, at the beginning of the day let all distraction and empty talk be silenced and let the first thought and the first word belong to him to whom our whole life belongs."\**

How does this reading enlighten the passage from Luke? Make sure to consider all three stories.

How does the biblical passage enlighten what Bonhoeffer wrote?

What experiences do you have of being silent before God and listening?

Bonhoeffer suggested the beginning of the day as the time to set aside all distraction and be silent before God. Do you think this would be helpful to you? What time would be best for you?

*Dietrich Bonhoeffer, *Life Together* (1954; gift edition, New York: HarperCollins, 1997), 37.

# 7. Partners

*Bible Story: Genesis 2:4b-25*

Sandra DeMott Hasenauer

### A Story behind the Story

This is a familiar story, and yet it is one that deserves deep study and reflection, particularly for youth who are still in the process of working out their understanding of their role in relationship to other people, to the world, and to God.

Genesis 2:4b-25 contains many key themes, but we will focus on only the three mentioned above. The first theme is that of *humans as created by God*. The word "formed" used to describe the creation of humanity (verse 7) is one that is usually found in the context of describing a potter (see Jeremiah 18:2-4). Picture God the artist, with mud-splattered hands, taking the time to sculpt the human in exactly the form God would deem "good." For youth, this might be the most difficult concept of the three to grasp. During a time when they are struggling with their self-image, they may find it challenging to consider themselves as God's work of art, and yet it is incredibly important that they do so.

The second theme is that of *humankind's role in taking care of the world*. God states that in the Garden of Eden the first couple were to "till it and keep it" (2:15). The word translated here as "till" is sometimes elsewhere translated as "serve," and in fact it is more frequently used in that sense (see Psalm 100:2, KJV, for example). We are to serve God's creation as part of God's created beings. More than seeing just a strong environmental message here, we are challenged to understand all of God's creation as intertwined together and to understand that our primary role as part of God's creation is to serve and guard the entire creation.

The third theme that this session will touch upon is *the relationship of person to person*. Who is supposed to have headship, based on the order of creation? Again, a word study is in order. The word that is used as "helper" in 2:18 does not mean "assistant" or "subordinate" or any other interpretation that would put man above woman. Rather, the word is most commonly used in reference to God—God as helper (see Psalm 121 for a well-known example). There is thus no evidence of a hierarchy, for surely God as helper is not subordinate in any way to humankind. The word is definitely that of a partnership, the couple lending support, companionship, and comfort to each other.

These few verses can offer much insight and challenge to our understanding of ourselves in relationship to God, to each other, and to all of creation. May we be open to the message God is sending us through these words.

### Enter the Story

Spend some time walking in the woods, or in a park with grass and trees, if you can. Perhaps you can watch a sunrise from your apartment window or look up into the sky a few times during the day. Visit a zoo or spend some time playing

- What does it mean to be God's work of art?
- How can I serve creation?
- How are men and women supposed to relate to each other?

## YOU MAY NEED

- modeling clay
- CD player and CDs of contemporary Christian music, for several options (all optional)
- several artistic depictions of the Creation story and of aspects of creation[1]
- short story based on the Creation story[2]
- newsprint or chalkboard
- markers and chalk
- Bibles
- "God's Work of Art" handouts
- writing utensils
- construction paper
- markers
- art supplies (such as glitter glue, art feathers, small pom-poms, foam shapes, etc.)
- "Trees and Rivers" handouts
- Bible study resources, such as commentaries on Genesis, concordances, Bibles with study notes, etc.
- Bible atlas[3]
- "Partners" story from the introduction to Marc Gellman's book *Does God Have a Big Toe?*[4] (optional)
- drawing and painting supplies, a chosen wall, other supplies as needed for a wall mural

with your pets. Discover a way to appreciate God's creation before you sit down to read this passage.

Once you've read Genesis 2:4b-25, reflect on your own relationship with creation. In what ways do you see yourself serving creation? Reflect on your relationship with other people: how are your relationships with people of the opposite gender a partnership or not a partnership? Do you need to make any adjustments there? (Especially consider how these relationships might be present in youth leadership, presenting examples to the youth in your ministry.) Finally, reflect upon your relationship with God. Do you have trouble considering yourself a work of God's art? Why or why not?

### Setting the Stage
### (5–10 minutes)
OPTION A
*Needed: modeling clay, CD player and CDs (optional)*
Give each youth a small lump or container of modeling clay as they enter the room, and invite them to be seated. Ask them to create an animal with their clay. It can be an animal of any sort—as long as it does not actually exist anywhere in the world! Yes, that's right, they are to create an entirely new animal, never before seen or even read about in fictional books (no unicorns allowed). Encourage them to have fun with their creations. Consider playing upbeat music in the background and setting an enjoyable mood in the room while they are sculpting. Remind them that lack of artistic talent doesn't matter; since no one has seen these animals before, no one would know what they're supposed to look like!

Once everyone has created an animal, tell the youth that they must now come up with a name for their species—the type of name that might show up in a textbook or on the label of a zoo enclosure. The name should somehow express the nature of the animal. When everyone has a name, take a few moments for the youth to introduce their new animal species to the rest of the class. Discuss:
- What clues did you use to help you decide on a name?
- Would you want the responsibility for naming all the animals in the world?

Let them know that today's story is about the creation of man and woman and about their role in the world.

OPTION B
*Needed: various artistic depictions of the Creation story and of creation*
Prior to the youth entering, lay the pictures of the Creation story and of creation along tables or in the center of the room where youth may observe each one easily. As youth enter, invite them to take several moments to walk through the room and look at each of the pictures quietly. Once everyone has had a chance to view the pictures, invite them to be seated. Ask them if they can discern a common theme of the pictures: what are they about? Invite the youth to each choose one piece of artwork that particularly strikes them in some way, but leave the artwork where it is. They should simply consider which is most meaningful to them.

After some discussion, let the group know that today's Scripture story is part of the story of Creation and that each of the pictures displayed depicts some aspect of creation. If you have time, invite the youth to share why they chose the artwork they did: what makes it meaningful to them?

## Telling the Story
## (5–10 minutes)
OPTION A
*Needed: story based on Creation story, Bibles*
Have the youth get comfortable, sitting as they choose to hear some wonderful stories. Take a few moments to share with them the story you have chosen, based on the Creation story. Remember, it need not be a direct retelling of the story; in fact, probably it would be better if it were not. Choose a story that will help them appreciate the Creation story in a different way. Some of the stories listed in endnote 2 will certainly help do this. Marc Gellman's short stories based on Bible stories are quite funny and yet still bring home the basic ideas of the original stories. Walter Wangerin's book is a gorgeous expression of God's love for us and of our part in the world. These or any other of your favorites will help the youth enjoy the Creation story in a different way than hearing it directly from the Bible.

After you've read the story of your choice, have the youth turn to Genesis 2:4b-25 and read it in the manner your group likes best. If you've got time, feel free to compare the biblical story with the story you shared first. How do they relate to each other? If you have even more time, feel free to share a second story with the youth. Then read the Genesis passage one more time. Compare the stories again.

OPTION B
*Needed: creation artwork from "Setting the Stage," Option B*
Invite the youth to each choose their favorite picture (the one that is most meaningful) on display and either stand near it or bring it to where they are seated. If more than one youth chooses the same picture, they may share it. Encourage the youth to continue to study the picture silently as you read to them Genesis 2:4b-25.

After they've heard the Scripture story, have them change pictures and find a different one. This should be one that did not immediately grab them or one they actually dislike for some reason. Again, they should bring it to where they are seated or stand near it, studying it, while you read the Scripture story to them again.

## Reacting to the Story
## (10–15 minutes)
OPTION A
*Needed: three sheets of newsprint, marker, Bibles*
Suggest to the youth that there are three main areas of the story that they will have the option of looking at during this session. On the top of the first newsprint, write, "Relationship between God and People." On the second newsprint, write, "Relationship of People to People." And on the third, write, "Relationship of People to the World."

Invite the youth to scan the story in their Bibles and see if they can find where each theme might be found in the story. Have them call out the Scripture citations for each one as they come across it (for example, one might suggest Genesis 2:7 for the theme of God and people). Have them think below the surface; it may not always be immediately obvious what theme a part of the Scripture could hold.

After the Scripture has been applied to the themes, have the youth brainstorm any questions, insights, or thoughts they might have about any of these themes. At this point, anything is fair game. If controversy arises, allow the youth to share their opposing views and then suggest that they might have the opportunity later in the session to research their questions further.

OPTION B

*Needed: artwork of the Creation story (from Options B above)*
After the youth have heard the Scripture while studying two different pictorial images of the Creation, have them return to their seats, if necessary. If you've got a larger group, consider breaking them into pairs or triads for the following discussion so that all will have a chance to share their responses. Invite the youth to discuss their experience, using questions like the following:
■ Why did you choose the first picture (the one you liked)?
■ How did it capture the idea of Creation for you?
■ What were you thinking about the picture as you heard the story read from the Bible?
■ Did it change the way you heard the story?
■ Why did you choose the second picture (the one you didn't like)?
■ What was it that you didn't like about the picture?
■ Did it *not* capture the idea of Creation for you? Why not?
■ What did you think about the picture as you were hearing the story a second time?

■ Did it change your opinion of the story?

## Connecting to the Story (10–15 minutes)
OPTION A
*(This option should be followed by Option A of "Exploring the Story.")*
*Needed: "God's Work of Art" handouts, writing utensils, CD player and quiet, meditative CDs (optional)*
Give each student a copy of the handout "God's Work of Art" and a writing utensil. Before giving them any further instruction, share with the youth the information from the second paragraph of "A Story behind the Story," which addresses the word *form*. (Of course, you should not include the comments about youth needing to hear this. Simply share the information about the word.) Next, ask a volunteer to read Jeremiah 18:1-4. Be sure to remind the youth that the Jeremiah passage is referring to the whole kingdom of Israel rather than to an individual person but that the imagery used is the same. Take a few moments to imagine out loud what a potter looks like while doing his work. Invite them to consider a potter's hands and concentration on the work.

After these images are in the students' minds, invite them to fill out Part A (and *only* Part A) of the handout at this time. You may want to play some quiet, meditative background music while they do their work.

OPTION B
*Needed: Bibles, newsprint, markers, "Partners" story from* **Does God Have a Big Toe?** *(optional)*
Remind the youth of the three themes of the Scripture story listed

56

above (if you did Option A of "Reacting to the Story;" if not, simply share the information about the three themes being present). Direct their attention to the second and third themes: (1) the relationship of people to people, and (2) the relationship of people to the world. Ask the youth to decide which theme interests them more as a class. There is the possibility of dividing into two groups, if the class does not overwhelmingly choose one theme.

Offer the information from "A Story behind the Story" on these two themes (whichever is chosen, or both), and invite volunteers to read the example Scriptures listed in the word study sections. Have the youth discuss their themes with this new understanding of the words. For example, how does it make the youth feel to think of themselves as serving God's creation? What other faith connections do they have with the word "servant"? Or how does it make them think of their friends or romantic relationships to think of themselves as partners? For the first theme, consider sharing the "Partners" story from the introduction of Marc Gellman's book *Does God Have a Big Toe?* and have the youth discuss it. For the second theme, there is a very funny depiction of the creation of Eve in a later story in the same book.

**Exploring the Story (10–15 minutes)**
OPTION A
*(This option follows Option A of "Connecting to the Story.") Needed: "God's Work of Art" handouts, writing utensils, Bibles,*

*construction paper, markers, art supplies*
Invite the youth to complete Part B of the handout and make their responses to the questions as thoroughly as they can. The answers to the questions are not always self-evident. The youth will need to do some reflecting. There are no "right answers," either. They may work in pairs or triads, but if doing so, the youth should follow this pattern: they should read the Scriptures together and perhaps discuss their responses to begin with, but they should do their own personal reflection when writing their responses on the handouts. Each of them may have a slightly different experience with this concept, and they should allow each other space for that. However, the conversations may also spur some support and encouragement between the youth as well. You may want to set the tone for these kinds of conversations in your own casual input into the groups' work.

After the youth have had sufficient time to complete Part B, make the construction paper, markers, and art supplies available, and instruct the youth to make themselves a poster of Psalm 139:14: "I praise you, for I am fearfully and wonderfully made." The poster should contain the words, and they may decorate them any way they choose. Encourage the youth to take these home with them and post them in a prominent place in their bedrooms.

OPTION B
*Needed: "Trees and Rivers" handouts, writing utensils, Bibles, Bible study helps, Bible atlas, markers, newsprint*

Give a copy of the "Trees and Rivers" handout and a writing utensil to each youth. Place various Bible study helps in the center of the room. Break into pairs, triads, or groups of four for this activity, depending on the size of your class. Invite the youth to complete the handout, using the helps available to them as they may need them. After they've completed the handout, have each small group create a poster, using the markers and newsprint, that would somehow illustrate a part of their study that they choose to focus upon. (One group may choose to do something with the four rivers, whereas another might choose the tree of life.) Allow enough time for the groups to display their posters for the rest of the class and to post them somewhere in the classroom. Also consider posting them in a location where they could be shared with the whole congregation.

## Living the Story (5–10 minutes)

OPTION A
*(This option may follow either option above.)*
*Needed: drawing and painting supplies, a chosen wall, other supplies as needed*
What a wonderful opportunity you now have to paint a full wall mural of the Creation story or some particular aspect of it. Choose a wall ahead of time, perhaps one of the walls in the youth room or in a hallway of the church. Be sure to plan well in advance so you allow enough time (possibly several weeks) for the completion of the project. Make sure all the youth are

somehow involved: some may sketch out the initial concept; others may trace that concept onto the wall. Obviously, everyone can be involved in the painting itself.

Be creative in the design. Perhaps the mural can move from images of the original Creation story through time along the length of the wall to images from today of God's continuing creation. Perhaps the design would focus on humankind's partnership with God in creation, or perhaps it would somehow lift up the two trees and the four rivers. For the particular "Living the Story" step for this session, you will have only enough time to announce the project and begin to spur ideas, and then you will need to close in prayer.

OPTION B
*(This option best follows Option B of "Exploring the Story.")*
*Needed: "Trees and Rivers" handouts, newsprint and markers or chalkboard and chalk (optional)*
Invite the youth to take a few moments to share their findings from their work prior to making the posters. Are there any disagreements as to what the rivers or either of the trees might mean? Take some time to discuss these findings, comparing and contrasting them without casting judgments in any way. Remind the class that scholars have been debating these same points for centuries. Ask the youth to consider, *If one of the valid interpretations of the rivers is that of God's sustenance, hope, and healing for the world, where do God's "rivers" need to flow today? In other words, what place in the world most needs*

*God's nourishment? God's hope? God's healing?* As youth share their responses, consider writing them on newsprint or a chalkboard. After this discussion, ask: *How can you help bring God's sustenance, hope, or healing to any of these places? Be specific.* Have the youth brainstorm their own possible involvement, and write these suggestions down as well.

Take a few moments to pray for these places and to pray for God's strength to be with us in our own involvement.

## Things to Ponder

There are several points at which youth may struggle with some of this session's concepts. Perhaps they are unsure of their relationship with the other gender. Or they may have difficulty picturing themselves as "wonderfully made." Or they may feel that *they* need God's hope and healing. Try to be aware of the various reactions to different parts of the discussions and follow up where you need to. Perhaps you could get adults in the church to start a letter-writing campaign to the youth, anonymously pointing out different positive qualities they see in the teens. (Be sure to inform the parents you're doing this ahead of time, however. In these times, a teenager getting an anonymous letter from an adult might cause concern.)

## Looking Ahead

There are several options in the next session that may require props for various activities. You will want to plan ahead in order to find anything you feel is appropriate. You may also need to find a video clip and a sound effects CD, as described in the session.

## Notes

1. Consider using posters or prints such as those at www.allposters.com (there is a category entitled "Biblical Scenes" under the religion section) or www.hollywoodjesus.com (in the "Store" section). Pictures should include those based on the biblical story itself as well as others that might simply be outdoor scenes, space shots of earth, and images of people. Try to include art from different traditions: classical Western, folk art, ethnic art, modern, etc. See if you can find a couple of examples that might feel jarring or unexpected to the youth.

2. Take the time to find a short story you really like. It need not be a direct retelling of the Creation story; it could be a piece of fiction based on the concept of the Creation story. Some good examples include the following: the story on pages 34–35 of Michael E. Williams, ed., *Genesis*, vol. 1 of *The Storyteller's Companion to the Bible* (Nashville: Abingdon, 1991); several stories from Marc Gellman, *Does God Have a Big Toe? Stories About Stories in the Bible* (New York: HarperCollins, 1989); and Walter Wangerin, *In the Beginning There Was No Sky* (Minneapolis: Augsburg, 1997).

3. The reference used in the preparation of the handout was G. Herbert May, ed., *Oxford Bible Atlas,* 3d ed. (New York: Oxford University Press, 1989).

4. Marc Gellman, *Does God Have a Big Toe? Stories About Stories in the Bible* (New York: HarperCollins, 1989).

# God's Work of Art

**Part A**

How am I God's work of art?

Is it hard to believe? Why?

Potters get personal with their work—their hands get dirty, they get splattered with wet clay, they concentrate completely on the clay in their hands until their creation is exactly the way they want it to be. How does it make you feel, thinking of God creating you in this same way? Why?

Does it make you feel different about yourself, knowing that God took such care and creativity with you? If so, why?

## Part B

*Read the following Scriptures:*

**Isaiah 43:1-7**      **Isaiah 44:21**      **Isaiah 64:8**      **Jeremiah 1:4-5**

What do you know about God now?

*Read Psalm 139.*

What do you know about God now?

What do you know about your relationship with God now?

*Read verse 14 again.*

How do you feel about that?

Is it hard to believe? Why or why not?

What can you do to help yourself believe this?

~~~~~~

# Trees and Rivers

**Part I**

We'll start with the slightly simpler one. If you were to look up the four rivers mentioned in Genesis 2:10-14 in a Bible atlas, you wouldn't find all of them. Check it out. If you've got an atlas, write here which rivers you can find mentioned:

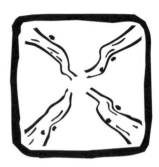

(Be careful! You might find something in the atlas with the same name, but it isn't a river!)

Now, what about the lands? Can you find them?

Great! Hopefully you found a few of them and located them on the map. What are some of these places called now?

Can you find one map that has several of the places on it? Get a feel for the area of the map that is covered by these few verses in Genesis.

To the people living in ancient times, this would have felt like the entire world to them. They didn't have the global experience that we do. Cush would have felt quite exotic and far away, for example. What do you think it meant to them that these four rivers flowed from the Garden of Eden? Can you describe God's relationship to the world based on these rivers?

Read Ezekiel 47:1-12 and Revelation 22:1-2. What do these rivers seem to symbolize? Do you think they're based on the rivers in Genesis? Why or why not?

## Part 2

This part is a little more difficult. The Tree of Life and the Tree of Knowledge have spurred arguments among Christians for generations. What are they? What do they symbolize? Why would eating of the Tree of Knowledge cause death?

The Tree of Life shows up a few times in Scripture. Check out Proverbs 11:30, 13:12, and 15:4. What is described as "a tree of life"?

Now read Revelation 2:7. What do you think the "tree of life" symbolizes here? You'll need to look beyond the obvious!

The Tree of Knowledge doesn't appear anywhere else in Scripture. You're on your own with this one. If you've got some commentaries on the Book of Genesis available, try reading the parts about the trees (most commentaries will be specific about which Scripture verses are covered in which sections). Make some notes here about what the trees might mean:

*Now it's your chance:*
What do you think the four rivers mean?

What do you think the Tree of Life means?

What do you think the Tree of Knowledge of Good and Evil means? (And why would eating of it cause you to "die"?)

What does all of this tell you about God and about your relationship with God?

# 8. The Flood

*Bible Story: Genesis 7–8*

**Paul Mast Hewitt**

## A Story behind the Story

Children are initiated into this well-loved story as pictures of arks and animals decorate their cribs and bedrooms. Yet in its familiarity some key details of this story may be lost. It is important to reexamine this story in its wider context, as part of the developing story of God's relationship with God's chosen people.

Chapters 7 and 8 of Genesis are those containing the story of the Flood itself. In it we discover that God directs Noah to bring aboard seven pairs of each clean animal and one pair of each unclean animal. This is probably different from what we remember of the story. (It is in Genesis 6 that God instructs Noah to put two of each animal on the ark.) What we have before us is apparently two different versions of the same story in oral tradition that the editor of the biblical story put together, ignoring some contradictory elements.

The Flood story, which begins in chapter 6 and concludes in chapter 9, occurs in the wider context of the story of Creation, Fall, and Redemption that makes up Genesis. The fall of humanity that began in chapter 3, with the eating of the forbidden fruit, is culminated in chapter 6 when God grieves over the wickedness of humanity. It is also the beginning of the covenant story in which God chooses a person, here Noah, through whom God will work to redeem creation. Later, God will also choose to work through others, such as Abraham. The Flood itself also brings us back to the beginning of Genesis, in which God separated the waters above from the waters below (Genesis 1:6-8). In the Flood story these waters break forth once more to return the earth to its original state of chaos.

All of this is in stark contrast to other flood stories that were present in the ancient Middle East. One such story is found as part of the epic of Gilgamesh and recounts the capricious acts of the gods and the heroic acts of one person, who eventually was granted immortality (see the "Another Flood Story" handout). For the biblical story, the perspective is very different. God is *always* in control and decides to flood the world, not because humanity has become too populous, but because humanity has become too sinful. In the midst of the storm God was not terrified but rather "remembered Noah" (Genesis 8:1). Noah is not the hero of the story; God is.

## Enter the Story

While this story is familiar to us as a children's story, it is important to revisit it and consider anew its meaning in the wider context of the biblical story and our story. As you read this story (you may want to read it beginning with chapter 6 and reading through chapter 9), take note of any questions and feelings you may have. Write them down. Let them settle in your thoughts and bring them to God in prayer. Questions you may want to consider include the following: What speaks to me? What disturbs me? How does this story intersect with my story?

## Setting the Stage
## (5–10 minutes)
OPTION A
*Needed: props for making the classroom into an ark, possibly including a recording of animal and storm sounds with a CD or tape player, wooden boards, bale of straw*

Before the youth arrive, set up the classroom as an ark. Your imagination and the time available are the only limits. Try to include props that impact as many of the five senses as possible. Ideas include:

- setting up a board or ramp at the doorway for youth to walk over to enter the "ark"
- bringing in a bale of straw for the smell as well as the sight (you will want to be sensitive to anybody with allergies)
- playing a recording of animal or storm sounds in the background
- posting pictures of animals on the walls or placing them on a table
- covering the windows with burlap to decrease the amount of light

As the youth arrive, include in your usual greeting talk about pets, favorite animals, and experiences with animals. Alternatively, you could talk about experiences with storms and how the youth feel about storms. Have they ever witnessed any truly frightening storms?

After a few minutes of general discussion, let the group know that this session's story is one that might be very familiar to them, but you will be looking at the story in its larger context and hopefully finding new meaning in it. Open with a brief time of prayer.

OPTION B
*Needed: artwork or other items that depict the ark*

Before the youth arrive, set up artwork or other items that depict the ark and the Flood. After your usual greeting of each youth, offer them an opportunity to talk about the flood story as they remember it. Do they remember when they first heard the story, or do they have other early memories of the ark or Flood story? You may choose to have them tell the story from beginning to end as they remember it. Does everybody remember the story the same, or are there discrepancies among different youths' telling? Does anyone know any songs about the ark story (such as "Rise and Shine" or "One More River to Cross")? Consider taking a moment to sing one together. Conclude your discussion with a brief introduction to the lesson of the day, and share in a brief time of prayer.

## Telling the Story
## (5–10 minutes)
OPTION A
*Needed: paper, writing utensils, Bibles*

Divide the youth into five groups, each of which will listen for something different while the story is read. If your group is small, individuals may work alone. If your group is large, you may want to keep the groups to a small size and have more than one group working on each listening item. Explain that each group will listen for one theme or idea as the story is read. As they

## POSSIBLE YOUTH CONTACT POINTS
- Did the Flood really happen?
- Does God care for the animals?
- Is God going to send another flood or some other punishment again?
- Does God protect us from the storms of life?
- Why did God send the Flood?
- Why did God demand the sacrifice of animals?

## YOU MAY NEED
- Bibles
- paper
- props for creating an "ark" atmosphere, possibly including wood, hay bales, etc.
- a tape or CD player with recordings of animal or storm sounds
- ark and flood artwork
- writing utensils
- crayons
- video of the Noah story with TV and VCR *or* a picture book of the story *or* a recording of Bill Cosby's "Noah" routine[1]
- newsprint or chalkboard
- markers or chalk
- index cards
- props for advertisement skits (any objects you feel are appropriate)
- "Another Flood Story" handouts
- "The Ancient Hebrew Worldview" handouts

hear references to that theme, they are to write down words or phrases to remind them of what was said. Give each person a piece of paper and a writing utensil.

Instruct Group 1 to listen for references to time and to keep track of how much time passes.

Group 2 should listen for references to animals. How many? What kinds?

Group 3 should listen to references to water. Where does it come from? Where does it go? How much is there?

Group 4 should listen for possible sounds and smells.

Group 5 should listen for possible feelings.

You may want to mention to these last two groups that they will be listening for things that are *implied* in the passage, not necessarily anything that is mentioned explicitly.

When everyone understands their assignments, read (or have read) Genesis 7–8 in its entirety. You may want to stop after a short portion to make sure everybody understands what they are supposed to be doing. This is followed up in Option A of "Reacting to the Story."

OPTION B
*Needed: video and VCR, picture book of the Flood story, or recording of Bill Cosby's "Noah" routine, CD player*
Before the class, obtain your choice of the suggested renditions of the flood story (video, audio, or book). (Note: If you chose the audio Cosby routine, you will want to choose ahead of time how much of the routine to hear; the entire piece is fairly long.) Have the youth watch or

listen to your choice of the above. After doing so, explain that they are now going to listen to the biblical account. As they are listening to the biblical story, they are to listen for similarities and differences between the two versions—the biblical one and the story or video version. Read (or have one or more of the youth read) Genesis chapters 7 and 8. This is followed up in Option B of "Reacting to the Story."

### Reacting to the Story (15–20 minutes)
OPTION A
*(Choose this option if you used Option A above.)*
*Needed: newsprint and markers or chalkboard and chalk*
After the story reading is finished, ask the youth if it was easy or difficult to listen in the way they were assigned. Were there differences in responses among the different groups? (Are facts easier to figure out than feelings, for example?) Have the various groups or individuals report on their listening activity, giving the information they gathered during their hearing. Be prepared to ask more questions to draw out details or explanations during each group's presentation.

After all the groups have reported, ask all of the youth the following questions:
■ What, if anything, surprised you?
■ What did you learn?
■ What questions were raised?

Write (or have one of the youth write) the group's responses on the newsprint or chalkboard. Let the group know that they will have time during the session to explore some of the questions as they may choose.

OPTION B
*(Choose this option if you used Option B above.)*
*Needed: newsprint and markers or chalkboard and chalk*
On the newsprint or chalkboard, make two columns, labeled "Differences" and "Similarities." Invite the youth to discuss the differences and similarities between the video, storybook, or comedy routine and the biblical story. While discussing, write the responses (or have one of the youth write them) on the newsprint or chalkboard. After everyone has had a chance to report on any differences or similarities, discuss the following questions:

■ What, if anything, surprised you when you heard the biblical story?

■ What did you learn?

■ Which was closer to what you remembered of the story: the storybook (or video or comedy routine) or the biblical version?

■ What questions were raised?

If you have time and the youth would like to, allow them to view the video, read the book, or listen to the comedy routine again, now that they've heard the biblical story as well. Let the group know that they will have time during the session to explore some of the questions as they may choose.

## Connecting to the Story (15–20 minutes)
OPTION A
*Needed: paper or index cards, writing utensils*
Hand out paper or an index card and a writing utensil to each person. Have the youth write on the paper one question they would ask God about this story. Have them place their questions on a pile in the center or at the front of the group. After all the questions have been placed in the pile, have each person pick a question without saying whether it is their question or not. (Some people may choose their own question, but as long as no one knows whose question it is, it remains anonymous.) Choose somebody to play the part of God. You may want to set aside one chair as "God's" chair or, alternatively, the youth may stay in their own seats. Have another youth read the question she or he picked. "God" is then to answer the question, as that person believes God might answer it. Encourage others to respond to "God's" answers. Does everyone agree that God would answer the question that way? What are other possible answers? After a question or two, choose another person to play the part of God. Continue as long as time allows or until all the questions have been discussed in this manner.

OPTION B
*Needed: paper, writing utensils, bag of props for each group of six*
Explain to the youth that they are going to have the opportunity to be part of the making of a new Noah movie—one based on the biblical account. If the group is large, youth can be divided into different teams of no more than six people. Each team is assigned the task of brainstorming for this movie the following questions:

■ What would be the focus of the movie?

■ How would it be different from the movie you watched (if you viewed a movie earlier in the session)?

- What would be the title?
- How would you market this movie to teens? (That is, why would teens want to go to this movie and how would you let them know that?)

Finally, they are to write the trailer or a TV advertisement for the movie targeting teenagers. You may want to have paper, pencils, and some props available for this part. If time allows, you may want each team to present their advertisement. They can either act it out or describe it.

## Exploring the Story (15–20 minutes)

If your group is large, you may want to assign half the group to do each of the following options. Afterward, be sure to have someone from each group summarize what they learned in his or her group.

### OPTION A
*Needed: "Another Flood Story" handouts*
Hand out copies of the "Another Flood Story" handout, which tells an ancient story of a flood similar to that of the biblical story. Read (or have someone read) the introductory paragraph aloud. Continue by having volunteers read the story. Discuss each question. If the group is large, you may want to separate into smaller groups for the discussion time to allow more people to participate directly. If you divide into smaller groups, have someone from each group report on what they learned in their group. Encourage them to find some creative way to make their report, if they can.

### OPTION B
*Needed: "Ancient Hebrew Worldview" handouts*
Make copies of the handout "Ancient Hebrew Worldview" for everybody. Explain that people over the years have imagined the universe in different ways and that, in fact, science continues to modify the way we understand the nature of the universe. Some Bible scholars believe the ancient Hebrews, including those who put our Scripture stories into writing, imagined the universe as it is pictured on the handout. The Bible frequently reflects this idea.

At this point you can divide into small groups of three to five learners, if you would like. Have them work through the instructions on the handout, discussing the answers in their groups. If time allows, ask one person from each group to report on their discussion. After they've done so, have the groups find a way to depict our current picture of the universe (using their bodies as the different elements, drawing on chalkboard or newsprint, etc.), and compare it with the ancient Hebrew perspective. What are the similarities? The differences? How does our worldview affect our understanding of the biblical flood story today?

## Living the Story (5–10 minutes)
### OPTION A
*Needed: paper, writing utensils, markers or crayons*
Writing in a journal can be one of the most helpful spiritual disciplines. The later teen years are a good time to begin to learn the art of journaling. If your group has a

tradition of keeping journals, use them for writing options such as this. If not, provide some blank paper to the youth and talk with them about journaling. Ask how many of them keep journals or diaries at home? What might make a spiritual journal different from a diary? Encourage them to begin such a practice (perhaps providing them with a journal to use), and let them know that writing on this paper now might be a start.

Invite the youth to reflect on the session, taking several minutes to journal about something in the story that connected with them. They could draw a picture, write a poem, write a prayer, or simply write something they learned this week. Have them find a quiet location to work on their reflections. After they have had a few minutes to work, encourage them to take their paper home, perhaps to begin their own journal, and close with prayer.

OPTION B
*Needed: paper or index cards, writing utensils*
Hand out the paper or index cards and writing utensils. Instruct the students to write down one question they have, or one thing they learned, from today's lesson. Make sure to tell them not to put their names on the cards, as what is written on there will be read aloud later. Give plenty of time for people to think.

After everyone has finished, have them place their papers in the center of the group. One by one, have people pick one and read it aloud, being careful not to disclose whether it is his or hers. If the youth have raised questions, spend a few moments brainstorming ways they might discover answers to (or at least research further) their questions. If they're not familiar with Bible study helps, take this opportunity to show them how to use concordances, commentaries, dictionaries, and encyclopedias, for example. End with a simple prayer, thanking God for what has been learned and lifting the questions before God.

## Things to Ponder
Questions about the historicity or geographic extent of the Flood may be raised during the course of this lesson. Do not avoid the questions, but be careful not to give a pat answer that will discourage further questioning. Questioning is an important part of the process of faith development. Furthermore, not even experts and theologians are in agreement on many of these questions. Encourage or provide time for the youth to discover their own answers to these questions by providing Bible study helps and assisting in their research.

## Looking Ahead
For the next session, there are several options for which you may need video clips or CDs. Be sure to read through the next session enough in advance to allow yourself time to locate all of the supplies you will want.

## Note
1. This routine can be found on *Bill Cosby Is a Very Funny Fellow: Right!* (Warner Brothers, rereleased on CD in 1995).

# Another Flood Story

*So, you thought the Bible was the only place a flood story was found? In fact, many cultures have flood stories that are similar to the Genesis story. Here is an ancient Middle Eastern story that comes from the eleventh tablet of the "Epic of Gilgamesh," a story in which the hero has many adventures as he seeks immortality. In this part of the story Gilgamesh finds the hero of the flood story, Utnapishti, who retells his own story to explain how he obtained immortality.*

The gods assembled and decided to send a deluge, a torrential storm. Among the gods were Enlil, Ea, the father of the gods Anu, and many others. Ea conspired to secretly tell a human, Utnapishti, of the gods' plans. Ea instructed Utnapishti to build a ship, equal on all sides and with a roof. Ea continued in his instructions by telling Utnapishti to abandon his own riches, seeking out all creatures of the earth and loading them into the vessel. Ea told Utnapishti to tell all the people that Enlil hated Utnapishti and Utnapishti must leave to avoid the wrath of Enlil. Furthermore, Utnapishti was to report that if he left, going to live instead in the lands of Ea, then Enlil would send down showers upon the people and they would have a wonderful harvest.

Utnapishti put the people to work building him a boat, and gathered to him all his silver and gold, loading it on the vessel. He also placed all the species of the animals into the vessel, and finally his family, kindred, and his craftsmen entered the boat. When Utnapishti saw the sky become stormy, he entered the boat also, and closed the doorway. The next morning, the storm god, Adad, began thundering within a black cloud. Other gods went forth ahead of the cloud and tore out all the irrigation dams. As the dark cloud of Adad passed over, no light could be seen. The gods themselves were frightened at the intensity of the storm, and fled to the heavens of Anu, hiding.

The storm blew on for six days and seven nights, the flood washing across the land. But on the seventh day, the storm began to subside. Utnapishti opened a vent and looked out to see a flat sea and realized that everyone had been killed. He bowed down and wept. He looked out again and saw mountain ranges had emerged from the water in twelve places and that the ship had run aground atop Mount Nisir. For seven days the ship stayed upon the mount without moving. Then Utnapishti let out a dove, but the dove came back for lack of a resting place. Then Utnapishti let out a swallow, which also returned. Finally, he set free a raven who did not return, having seen that the earth was returning to its natural state. When the raven disappeared,

*Adapted from J. V. Kinnier Wilson, trans., "The Story of the Flood," in *Documents from Old Testament Times*, D. Winton Thomas, ed. (New York: Harper & Row, 1958), 17–26.

Utnapishti set free all the animals and made a food-offering to the gods, who then gathered at the smell of the incense. But Enlil was angry that something had survived the deluge. Ea spoke against Enlil for indiscriminately destroying the whole of humankind and counseled him, instead, to send forth plagues that would diminish but not destroy humankind. Enlil then went to Utnapishti and his wife and blessed them, granting them immortality.*

**What do the two stories have in common?**

**How does this story portray the gods differently from the biblical story's portrayal of God?**

**Who acted heroically?**

**What other differences between the two stories help you understand the Genesis story better?**

∿∿∿∿∿

# The Ancient Hebrew Worldview

*The Bible comes from a prescientific worldview. Many biblical scholars believe the biblical writers imagined the universe as pictured below:* *

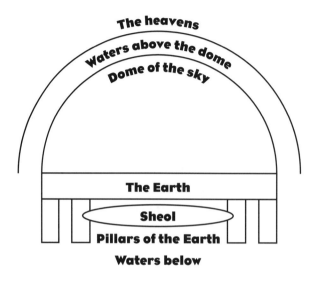

*Discuss the following questions:*

Read Genesis 1:6-10. What evidence in these verses do you see for this view of the universe?

What connections can you make between these verses from the Creation story and the Flood story?

If this were the worldview of the biblical writers, how might that affect your understanding of what happened in the Flood?

How might it affect your understanding of the meaning of the Flood?

*Adapted from Henry Jackson Flanders, *People of the Covenant* (New York: Oxford University Press, 1988), 95.

# 9. The Ten Commandments

*Bible Story: Exodus 20:1-21*

Lisa and Chris Holliday

### A Story behind the Story

Throughout the Old Testament we find the word *covenant*. A covenant is a solemn promise or an agreement, and often it reveals a tremendous amount about the relationship between the covenant makers. In accordance with the covenant that God made with Abraham (Genesis 12, 15, 17), God frees the Israelites from the Egyptians.

After Moses and the Israelites cross the Red Sea, they begin their journey in the wilderness. Three new moons after leaving Egypt, the Israelites enter the wilderness of Sinai, where they set up camp at the foot of the mountain (Exodus 19:1). This mountain becomes a place of mystery and wonder for the people, and a place of divine meeting and covenant.

God calls to Moses from the mountain and instructs him to tell the people, "You have seen what I did to the Egyptians, and how I bore you on eagles' wings and brought you to myself. Now therefore, if you obey my voice and keep my covenant, you shall be my treasured possession out of all the peoples. Indeed, the whole earth is mine, but you shall be for me a priestly kingdom and a holy nation" (Exodus 19:4-6). Once Moses tells the Israelites these things, God has him ready the people for their meeting with God.

After a time of preparation, the Israelites gather at the foot of the mountain. At the beginning of chapter 20, God speaks. Scholars debate whether 20:18-21 (when the people are frightened and ask Moses to be their mediator) should be where it is or at the end of chapter 19, which would place it before the Ten Commandments. Either way, most agree that God's commandment speech "is the only speech heard directly by Israel. The [Ten Commandments] thus are unique as 'direct revelation.' . . . Commandments given subsequently by the mediator will be important, but cannot rival in authority this direct address, which constitutes the core of Yahweh's intent and charter for Israel's covenantal existence."[1]

Most people divide the Ten Commandments into two major sections: "one concerning relations to God (vv. 1-11), and one concerning the neighbor (vv.12-17)."[2] After the Ten Commandments are received, God gives more laws. Then, in chapter 24, the people agree to obey "all the words that the LORD has spoken" (verse 3) and they participate in a ceremony to seal the covenant.

### Enter the Story

Find a Bible that has section titles and look through Exodus to get an idea of the flow of events. Take time to read chapters 19, 20, and 24. Think about what Moses and the Israelites must have felt. Consider how you feel talking with God as compared to the way the Israelites did. Maybe the images

## POSSIBLE YOUTH CONTACT POINTS

- How do I honor my parents considering . . . ?
- I work a part-time job on Sunday. Am I breaking one of the commandments?
- How do I use God's name inappropriately?
- What idols and other gods do I have in my life?
- Are the commandments relevant to my life?
- How do I live each one of these commandments, really?

## YOU MAY NEED

- Bibles
- TV and VCR
- video that portrays the Israelites crossing the Red Sea
- trumpet or drum and a person to play the instrument
- sign that reads, "Mount Sinai"
- newsprint and markers
- Bible study resources
- pencils
- blank paper
- colored pencils, thin markers, or crayons
- recording of Exodus 20:1-21 on CD or tape
- the sounds of a storm with thunder on CD or tape
- strobe light
- "The Ten Commandments" handouts
- CD or tape player
- contemporary Christian CDs or tapes with some meditative songs on them[3]
- party hats
- ten wacky rules on newsprint or poster board (at least two copies)
- ten folded pieces of paper with one commandment on each
- basket or hat
- "My Covenant with God" handouts
- closing hymn or chorus

of God portrayed here do not match your current images. The youth may feel this too. Give yourself some time to reflect on the personality of God.

As you read the Ten Commandments, consider each one and think about how it applies to your life. What are your idols? Do you covet in any ways? How does the Sabbath commandment apply to your life? What does God expect of you? What are you willing to agree to do or not do for God?

What about honoring parents? Leaders and youth may particularly struggle with this one. Families are quite diverse in our culture, and abuse and neglect are common. Help your youth as they consider who their parents are and what honoring them in safe and appropriate ways means for them. Throughout your reflection, talk to God and listen for what God might communicate to you.

## Setting the Stage (5–10 minutes)

OPTION A
*Needed: TV and VCR, video that portrays Israelites crossing the Red Sea, musical instrument and instrumentalist, "Mount Sinai" sign*

Before the class starts: (1) Decide on a confusing maze route through the building or outside. (2) Preset the video clip of the Israelites crossing the Red Sea from a movie such as *The Ten Commandments* or *The Prince of Egypt*. (3) Have someone in your class be prepared to play a short fanfare, the "charge" cheer, or a loud drum roll on a musical instrument.

Begin the class by showing the video clip of the crossing. As the clip ends, have your musician surprise everyone with the fanfare. Right after he or she finishes, shout, "The Lord has delivered us! We have crossed the Red Sea. Let us set out into the wilderness. Follow me!"

Lead the youth through the maze and end in your usual gathering space—or in a different place, like the sanctuary. Have a sign posted at the end that reads, *Mount Sinai.* Act as if you are Moses and tell the youth that they have arrived at Mount Sinai. Briefly summarize information from "A Story behind the Story" and Exodus 19. End by inviting them to gather at the foot of the mountain to hear the word of God.

OPTION B
*Needed: two copies of ten wacky rules on newsprint, blank newsprint, party hats*

Before the session, post ten wacky rules at your space's entrance and inside your space. Examples:
- Thou shalt not use your hands.
- Thou shalt not *not* wear a party hat.
- Thou shalt eat ten M&Ms (you could spread M&Ms on a table).
- Thou shalt talk only about the topic your leader yells out (ice cream, movies, etc.).
- Thou shalt greet each other by shaking feet.
- Thou shalt not sit down.

As the youth arrive, ask them to agree to follow the rules until you give them a special signal (such as flashing the lights). After the youth have all had a chance to participate, give the signal and ask them to have a seat.

Talk about the silly rules that they have been following. Then ask them for rules that apply to their lives and list them on newsprint. You could broaden this to the general laws of society. Ask what they like about specific rules and what they don't like. Ask if we need rules, and why or why not? Tell them that the group is going to be discussing ten famous laws that God gave us, called the Ten Commandments.

## Telling the Story
## (5–10 minutes)
OPTION A

*Needed: CD or tape player, Exodus 20:1-21 on CD or tape, sound effects of storm with thunder on CD or tape, strobe light, Bible*
Before the session, record two people reading Exodus 20:1-21. Have a narrator read verses 1 and 18-21. Have another person read verses 2-17. You could also incorporate a CD with storms and thunder on it as background on the recording. Or you could use a professional recording of the Bible, preferably one with sound effects included. (If you don't a have a professional recording, you could make your own.)

Dim the lights and have the group stand together in the center of the room. Start the tape. As the students listen, turn on a strobe light or flash the lights on and off to simulate lightning. At the conclusion of this experience, turn the lights back on and have the students sit down. At this point you may choose to have someone read the Scripture or play the tape again

with the students sitting quietly and the lights on.

## OPTION B
*Needed: Bibles*
Have everyone turn in their Bibles to Exodus 20:1-21. If needed, summarize information from "A Story behind the Story" and Exodus 19. This information sets the stage for the Ten Commandments and will help the youth put the Scripture into context. Ask the students to follow along in their Bibles as a few students read the Scripture.

After hearing the Scripture, ask the students to talk about times when they have witnessed storms, earthquakes, fires, etc. Encourage them to use those images as they listen to the Scripture a second time.

Dim the lights and invite the students to close their eyes. (If you choose, you might encourage them to spread out in the room so everyone has space.) Instruct the youth to pretend that they are the Israelites. The Lord has delivered them from the Egyptians, and they have seen many miracles of God: the plagues God sent upon the Egyptians, the parting of the Red Sea, and the gift of bread from the sky. They have even seen water flow from a rock.

Now, ask the youth to picture themselves at the foot of Mount Sinai. Invite them to imagine the thunder, the lightning, the fire, and the shaking earth. Ask them to picture the cloud of smoke all around the mountain and to imagine hearing the voice of God speak these words. Read the passage, giving it as much drama as you feel comfortable doing.

**Reacting to the Story
(15–20 minutes)**

OPTION A

*Needed: newsprint and markers*

As a group, discuss the following questions:

■ How did you feel as you listened to the Scripture?

■ Describe the mental pictures you saw as you heard the Scripture.

■ How do you think the Israelites felt as they stood at the foot of the mountain?

■ Is "commandments" a good word to describe this passage? Why or why not?

Next, label a sheet of newsprint with the title "Images of God." Ask the class:

■ What images do you have of God?

■ How would you describe God?

Write their responses on the newsprint. Indicating the list, ask the youth to consider which images of God stand out to them in the Scripture. Circle the ones the youth choose.

After doing so, discuss the story using the following questions:

■ How does the Scripture make you feel about God?

■ Why does God ask the Israelites to follow these commandments?

■ Do you think we are supposed to follow them too? Why or why not?

■ Toward the end of the passage, the people ask Moses to be their mediator. Why do they do this?

■ Do we have others talk to God for us today? Do we talk to God ourselves? If so, compare how you feel when you talk to God compared to how you think the Israelites felt.

OPTION B

*Needed: colored pencils, thin markers or crayons, blank paper*

Make the supplies available, and invite each youth to draw a picture that represents the scriptural event they have heard. Have them consider the different people who were present, the environment, and the picture of God portrayed.

As they are completing the first drawing, invite them to use a second sheet of paper to create a picture of themselves talking with God, and ask them to show both themselves and a representation of God in the picture. Ask the youth to think about where they communicate with God and what that experience is like for them.

After both drawings are complete, have all the students share their pictures and respond to the drawings as a group. Then, again as a group, discuss the difference or similarity between the Israelites' experiences with God and our own.

**Connecting to the Story
(15–20 minutes)**

OPTION A

*Needed: Bibles, "The Ten Commandments" handouts, writing utensils, newsprint and markers, meditative contemporary Christian CD or tape, CD or tape player*

Pass out "The Ten Commandments" handouts and writing utensils. Ask the group to name the Ten Commandments and to write them on their handouts as you write them on newsprint. Then, as you play some meditative contemporary Christian music, invite the youth to complete the handout questions about each commandment. Invite them to consider what each commandment meant to the Israelites and what it means to them today.

After they have completed "The Ten Commandments" handouts, divide the youth into small groups and ask them to discuss their responses. Have each group select a reporter to summarize and write down the group's thoughts, and give the reporter a blank handout to use for that purpose. After the youth have had time to share in their small groups, gather them all back together and have each reporter talk about the group's responses to the handout questions.

OPTION B

*Needed: newsprint and markers, ten folded scraps of paper with one commandment on each, basket*

As a group, name the Ten Commandments and list them on a sheet of newsprint. Then divide the youth into pairs or small groups. Take the basket of folded scraps of paper and ask each group to draw out one or more pieces of paper, depending on how many groups you have. Try to ensure that all ten of the commandments are covered. Learners will be performing skits based on these commandments. Ask each group to keep their commandment(s) secret until their performance time.

Before this exercise, make sure you have enough rehearsal spaces prepared so that each group can practice in a somewhat private space. Invite each group to go and rehearse a one-minute example of breaking that commandment in

today's world (one example per selected commandment). Ask them to concentrate on real-life situations involving teens and young adults.

After some rehearsal time, gather the large group back together and allow each small group to perform their skit(s). After each commandment skit, have the large group guess which commandment was broken. Then lead the youth in a discussion about other ways people of today break that commandment. Also consider ways that people keep the commandment and encourage the youth to give specific examples.

## Exploring the Story (15–20 minutes)

OPTION A

*Needed: paper, pencils, newsprint of the commandments, newsprint and markers, Bibles with concordances or Bibles and separate concordances*

Have the youth divide into pairs, and give each pair a blank sheet of paper. Have the newsprint with the commandments written on it visible to the youth.

Ask each pair to rank the commandments in order of importance, with the most important being number one and the least important being number ten. After they have done so, come back together as a large group and let one member of each pair vote the pair's rankings. Use the newsprint with the commandments on it to tally the voting, and write the appropriate ranking number beside each commandment. Ask the youth:

- Was it difficult to decide which was most important?
- How did you decide? What criteria did you use?

Tell the youth that Jesus, too, was asked which commandment was the greatest. His response is recorded in the Bible. Help them discover where that passage might be. Help them narrow it to the Gospels, then have them look in a concordance for key words such as *commandments* or *first*. If they cannot find it, inform them that it is in Matthew 22:34-40 and Mark 12:28-31.

Jesus has summarized all the commandments by his response. Ask the youth:

- Which two commandments did Jesus choose?
- Do the rest of the commandments fit into these two categories?
- Are any commandments specifically about our relationship to God? If so, which ones?
- Are any specifically about our relationship to our neighbors? If so, which ones?
- Do any have to do with loving ourselves, since we are supposed to love our neighbors as ourselves? If so, which ones and how do they apply in this way?

OPTION B
*Needed: paper, writing utensils, Bibles, Bible study resources*
Make sure each youth has a blank piece of paper, a pencil or pen, and a Bible. Using Bible study resources, such as concordances, study Bibles, Bible dictionaries, and commentaries, invite the youth to explore the word *covenant*. You could break them into groups of two or three or allow them to work alone. Ask each group or individual to write a definition of covenant. Also invite them to look specifically at the covenants made between God and the Israelites. Have them write out a time line of major covenant events beginning with Abraham and ending with Exodus 24:1-8. A Bible with section titles will be most helpful in the time line process.

**Living the Story
(5–10 minutes)**
OPTION A
*Needed: "The Ten Commandments" handouts, writing utensils, meditative contemporary Christian CD or tape, closing hymn or chorus*
Invite each youth to take their handout and a writing utensil to a quiet place apart from everyone else. Instruct the youth to pick two commandments that they are willing to make an extra effort to follow this week. Have them turn their handouts over to the back, write one commandment at the top of the page, and write the other in the middle. Under each, they should write specific ways they plan to follow these commandments during the week. Invite them to pray about these choices and to ask God for help. You could play some meditative contemporary Christian music throughout this section.

After an appropriate length of time, gather the group together and form a circle. Sing a chorus or hymn such as "Awesome God" or "I Have Decided to Follow Jesus." Then offer a closing prayer in which you pray for the youth and their new commitments.

OPTION B

*Needed: "My Covenant with God" handouts, writing utensils, meditative contemporary Christian CD or tape, closing hymn or chorus*

Pass out the "My Covenant with God" handouts. Tell the youth that throughout the Bible, God promised Abraham and the Israelites many things and that, as people of God, we too can trust in God and God's promises. Tell them that the Scriptures listed on the handout are just a few of the many promises of God. Point out the passage in which the Israelites promised to obey God's commandments, in Exodus 24:1-8.

Invite each youth to complete the handout. Help the youth reflect individually on the following:

■ Am I willing to obey the Ten Commandments?

■ Am I willing to live in the ways of God?

■ What do these things mean to me, and to what am I willing to commit?

Encourage each youth to end their time with silent prayer.

If some want to make covenants, they are welcome to do so, but let the youth know that there is no pressure. You could play some meditative contemporary Christian music throughout this section.

End by bringing the whole group together in a circle. Affirm the youth for taking time to consider making a covenant with God and encourage them to continue thinking about what the Ten Commandments and covenant mean for their lives. Close by singing a hymn or chorus together as your final prayer.

## Things to Ponder

Consider which activities worked best for your youth group. This will help you select learning options for them in the future. Also, are there issues that arose during the session that need further discussion with individuals or with the group? Are any of the youth struggling with any of the commandments or with the idea of covenant? Take time this week to pray for each youth and be ready to follow up with them as appropriate. You may want to keep a journal in which you reflect on each youth session and each significant youth interaction.

## Looking Ahead

You may need to find some basic information on church reformation movements, particularly within your own denomination. A good place to start is by looking up Martin Luther online or in a children's encyclopedia. You might also be able to find information on Vatican II or on Henry VIII and the Church of England. You may also need to find resources that will help the youth consider where faith and politics intersect, if at all. Finally, you may want to invite your pastor or a church elder to the class.

## Notes

1. Walter Brueggemann, *The Book of Exodus: Introduction, Commentary, and Reflections*, vol. 1 of *The New Interpreter's Bible: A Commentary in Twelve Volumes* (Nashville: Abingdon, 1994), 854.
2. Ibid., 839.
3. Music artists who have appropriate meditative music include Michael W. Smith, Steven Curtis Chapman, and Jaci Velasquez.

# The Ten Commandments

**First Commandment** _____

What do you think this commandment meant for the Israelites?

How does it apply to you, or what does it mean for you?

**Second Commandment** _____

What do you think this commandment meant for the Israelites?

How does it apply to you, or what does it mean for you?

**Third Commandment** _____

What do you think this commandment meant for the Israelites?

How does it apply to you, or what does it mean for you?

**Fourth Commandment** _____

What do you think this commandment meant for the Israelites?

How does it apply to you, or what does it mean for you?

**Fifth Commandment** _____

What do you think this commandment meant for the Israelites?

How does it apply to you, or what does it mean for you?

**Sixth Commandment** _____

What do you think this commandment meant for the Israelites?

How does it apply to you, or what does it mean for you?

**Seventh Commandment** _____

What do you think this commandment meant for the Israelites?

How does it apply to you, or what does it mean for you?

**Eighth Commandment** _____

What do you think this commandment meant for the Israelites?

How does it apply to you, or what does it mean for you?

**Ninth Commandment** _____

What do you think this commandment meant for the Israelites?

How does it apply to you, or what does it mean for you?

**Tenth Commandment** _____

What do you think this commandment meant for the Israelites?

How does it apply to you, or what does it mean for you?

# My Covenant with God

**Scripture:**
**Isaiah 41:10**

God's promise to me is . . .

**Scripture:**
**Jeremiah 29:11-14**

God's promise to me is . . .

**Scripture:**
**Hebrews 13:5**

God's promise to me is . . .

**Scripture:**
**Isaiah 54:10**

God's promise to me is . . .

**Dear God,**

**I promise . . .**

_____

_____

_____

_____

_____

_____

_____

_____

_____

_____

_____

_____

_____

_____

_____

_____

# 10. Josiah's Reform

*Bible Story: 2 Kings 22*

Sandra DeMott Hasenauer

### A Story behind the Story

Together, the books of 1 and 2 Kings form a history of a particular time in the life of Israel. However, this is not history the way you read it in your high school textbooks. This is history with a point. The stories in these two books are a meditation upon the role of a God who is active in the events of history and active in the daily experiences of the chosen people. Years after these events occurred, the people looked back upon them and asked, "Why?" The answer they determined is "Because God ordained it to be so." This is equally true for positive and negative events.

The story is seen from the standpoint of the fall of Jerusalem, involving the destruction of the temple, in 587 BCE. In fact, the story is shaped in many ways around the temple itself. After David's death, his son Solomon comes to reign. Solomon proclaims his faith by building the house of the Lord (see 1 Kings 6–8). The building of the temple and its consecration are described in great detail. In 2 Kings 25, great attention is given to the destruction of the temple as the people are being exiled to Babylon. The temple itself is a symbol of God's presence in the midst of God's people. It also becomes a bellwether for describing the people's faithfulness to God. Solomon is faithful and builds the temple. Solomon falls by the wayside (1 Kings 11), and the story goes downhill from there. By the time we reach King Josiah, the temple has fallen into such disrepair that Josiah needs to pay great sums of money to fix it up.

Josiah's story stands side by side with Solomon's, almost as a "good king/bad king" scenario. Josiah, the good king, is noted as being faithful his entire life, wavering neither "to the right or to the left" (2 Kings 22:2). He was prepared to hear the Word of God (in the finding of the scroll), felt it convict his people's lack of faith, and did everything in his power to bring his people onto the right path. Unfortunately, the die had already been cast. Jerusalem was doomed to downfall. The temple would be destroyed and the people taken into exile. According to the biblical historian, the generations of disobedience were too much to be overcome by one king's reign.

### Enter the Story

If you have time, read all of 1 and 2 Kings so you can get a feel for the whole sweep of history. Also, consider your own church tradition. Is your denomination a reform movement of another denomination? Almost everyone's is. Even Roman Catholics have felt the winds of reform through Vatican II. What do you know about church reform?

What do you know about personal reform? Have there been times in your life when you discovered you were heading down the wrong path and needed to redirect yourself? Have you ever gone through a time of true repentance? What did that process of repentance look like in your life? Consider all these things as you begin your reading of the story for this session.

## Setting the Stage
## (5–10 minutes)
OPTION A
*Needed: dusty old book with the title obscured*

After youth enter the classroom and you've had some time to do some checking in, hold up a really old, tattered, dusty book with the title obscured from the youth's vision. Make sure your voice sounds a little excited, a little apprehensive. Make up a story about having to help out in cleaning some area of the church to make repairs and coming across this book. Explain to the youth that you spent some time over the last few days reading this book and discovered that it tells you exactly how the church should be doing everything—and that the church has been doing it wrong! When the youth start asking questions, keep your story vague, but build up the emotions—perhaps you could even start sounding really upset about the mistakes you've been making. Obviously, the youth won't believe a word you're saying, but go ahead and ham it up anyway.

After a few minutes, tell them that today's Scripture story is about someone who was making repairs to the temple and found a copy of part of the Bible that hadn't been seen for an awfully long time. When they read it, they realized how far away from God they'd moved. Ask the youth to consider how they might feel if they found something like that.

OPTION B
*Needed: newsprint and marker or chalkboard and chalk, brief information on church reform movements of history*

After the youth enter, spend some time checking in with them on the events of their lives since they were last together. Then invite the youth to identify times of reform in church history. Have them call out names (such as Martin Luther, Henry VIII, or more recent examples from your own tradition) or periods of history, and list these on the newsprint or chalkboard. If the youth are clueless, tell them the basic details of the Lutheran reformation, the beginning of the Anglican Church, or any history from your own church tradition.

Ask the youth to define the word *reform*. Write this definition on the newsprint or chalkboard. Inform the class that today's Scripture story is about a reform of the temple in ancient times.

## Telling the Story
## (5–10 minutes)
OPTION A
*Needed: "And the Scripture Says . . ." handouts, writing utensils, Bibles*

Give each youth a copy of the "And the Scripture Says . . ." handout and a writing utensil. Invite them to fill in the handout as you are reading the passage—the answers to most of the questions are in the reading itself. You will want them to focus only on questions 1–22 at this time. This is not a test; it is simply a way to help the youth sort through some of the more complex parts of the passage and to focus on the central ideas.

After you've read the entire Scripture, allow the youth a couple of moments to finish filling in the answers to the questions as best they can. You may need to read through a section again if they

## POSSIBLE YOUTH CONTACT POINTS
- How do I repent?
- How does faith intersect with government?
- Am I being truly faithful?

## YOU MAY NEED
- dusty old book with the title obscured
- newsprint and marker or chalkboard and chalk
- brief information on church reform movements of history[1]
- "And the Scripture Says . . ." handouts
- writing utensils
- Bibles
- costumes and props (optional)
- blank or lined notebook paper
- "Ready to Hear" handouts
- youth-appropriate resources on the relationship between faith and politics, plus statements from your denomination on the intersection of faith and politics (optional)
- pastor or elder (optional)
- worship planning resources
- hymnals or songbooks

request it. Try to refrain from simply giving them the answers outright—reread the appropriate sections until they pick up on the answers themselves.

After they have questions 1–22 completed, invite them to take their best shot at answering the two questions under "Your Own Thoughts." This will help them pick up on a couple of the main themes of the story.

OPTION B
*Needed: Bibles, costumes and props (optional)*
Ask for volunteers to mime the actions of the characters in this story as you read it. They need not rehearse ahead of time; in fact, it would be more enjoyable for the class to simply have the volunteers act out their roles as they hear them. You will need, at least, persons to play Josiah, Shaphan, Hilkiah, and Huldah. If you would like to have everyone in the class involved, you could also have some mime the workers in the temple and the servants Ahikam, Achbor, and Asaiah. If you have some props and costumes, make them available to your actors. You may want to have a piece of scrap fabric available for Josiah to tear in place of his clothes. Roll up a piece of paper to use as the "book of the law" that is found in the temple. (Remember, in ancient times books were scrolls.) Encourage the youth to have fun with the story and yet still try to find the basic themes of it.

**Reacting to the Story (10–15 minutes)**
OPTION A
*(This option follows Option A of "Telling the Story.")*

*Needed: "And the Scripture Says . . ." handouts, Bibles, newsprint and marker or chalkboard and chalk (optional)*
Have the youth get into pairs if you have a larger class. Spend several moments going over the responses to the questions on the "And the Scripture Says . . ." handout—in pairs or as a class. Allow the youth to share the answers, and discuss any that might be of particular interest to them. (For example, it might be fun to compare their lives as eight year olds with Josiah's as an eight year old.) If any questions come up about the text, feel free to write these down on newsprint or chalkboard for reference later. Come back to the list at the end of class, if you have time, to see what questions were answered or if new questions arose during the session. Do not feel as though you have to answer all questions yourself. Remember, the youth are the interpreters, so your job may simply be to help them figure out where they could find responses to their questions.

OPTION B
*(This option follows Option B of "Telling the Story.")*
*Needed: Bibles*
Have the youth discuss for a few moments what their character may have been thinking, feeling, or worried about during the different parts of the story. For example, ask the volunteer who portrayed Josiah to consider how he might have felt at eight, beginning to reign over a country. Once "Josiah" has had a chance to respond, invite the rest of the class to offer their opinions as well. If they were Josiah at eight, how would they feel? Go through

each character, and each part of the story, inviting first the person who portrayed that character, and then the rest of the class, to consider what their thoughts or actions might have been if they were living through those events. Consider, also, what motivations might be behind actions—we're not often given this information in Scripture. For example, why would Hilkiah have thought to mention the found book to Shaphan the secretary? Why did Shaphan decide to bring it to the king? What might Shaphan have been thinking on the way to see the king, to announce the finding of the book? Use questions like these for each character, to help the youth flesh out the story for themselves in human terms.

## Connecting to the Story (10–15 minutes)

OPTION A
*Needed: Bibles, paper, writing utensils, newsprint and markers*
Invite the youth to read verse 11 again. Ask the youth to discuss: *What do you think made Josiah tear his clothes when he heard the word of the law read to him?* Encourage the youth to consider Josiah's actions as those of a repentant sinner. Josiah has just heard the law, which his people have not been following well throughout their history. Ask: *How do you think Josiah would have felt, hearing God's commands repeated to him now? Why?* Invite the youth to brainstorm situations in which teenagers like themselves might feel repentant. (If you need to, define the word *repentant*.) Asking the question like this allows a certain amount of distance from the question, and hope-

fully the youth will feel comfortable answering in a more hypothetical situation. List some of these situations on newsprint, inviting discussion for each situation listed in terms of why repentance would be needed, from whom forgiveness needs to be asked, and how true repentance might be shown. Invite discussion, also, on the difference between true repentance and false repentance.

Once the youth seem to have a pretty good hold on what repentance is and how it might be felt, make sure each youth has paper and writing utensils and encourage them to find a quiet, private space and write for a few moments about an area in their life for which they would like to ask God's forgiveness. They may also wish to write a prayer of repentance.

OPTION B
*Needed: "Ready to Hear" handouts, writing utensils, Bibles*
Give each youth a copy of the handout "Ready to Hear," and make sure they each have a writing utensil. If you feel your class would work better in pairs, divide them up as such. Remind the groups that the final paragraph is to be private, individual work and they need to give each other some space and undistracted time to complete the reflections there.

## Exploring the Story (10–15 minutes)

OPTION A
*Needed: youth-appropriate resources on faith and politics, along with statements from your denomination on the intersection of faith and politics (optional)*

Take a few moments to remind the youth that at the time in Israel's history when the story of King Josiah takes place, the monarchy is very much a religious institution. Faith and politics are tightly intermingled, and, in fact, no division is seen between them at all. Rather, the king is anointed by God and is supposed to carry out God's word.

Invite the youth to take a moment or two to lift up other current examples of places where faith and politics are mixed. Are there any places where faith and politics are completely separate? (The answer to this might not be as obvious as it seems.) If you have access to any resources on the intersection of faith and politics that you would like to share with the class at this time, do so. If your class really enjoys in-depth, topical discussions, this is a perfect opportunity to have a good discussion of the relationship between government and faith.

Consider using such questions as the following to help spur discussion, but don't feel chained to the questions—the youth may have some insightful comments to make, and the discussion might take a completely different turn.

■ Do you feel that faith has any place in politics? Why or why not?

■ What does it mean to you to hear that a presidential candidate is a faithful churchgoer?

■ How comfortable would you be if a president from a different faith (Jewish, Muslim, or Buddhist) were to be elected? Why?

■ What does your own faith tell you about your politics? Has it affected your choice (or the choice you think you will eventually make) about joining a political party? Should it?

If your denomination has any particular resources related to its stand on faith and politics, share them with the youth and invite discussion of these resources, as well.

OPTION B

*Needed: Bibles, newsprint, markers*

Have the youth read 2 Kings 23:1-25 and list on newsprint all of the reforms that occurred under King Josiah. Compare 2 Kings 22 with Deuteronomy 6:4-5 (especially if you did Option B of "Connecting to the Story"). Ask:

■ How was Israel disobeying the commandment in Deuteronomy 6:4-5?

■ What other "gods" do we worship today? (That is, what do we center our lives on other than God?)

## Living the Story (5–10 minutes)

OPTION A

*Needed: church pastor or elder (optional)*

Invite the youth to consider your own church and denomination. Are you part of a reform tradition? If so, present some of that history briefly to the class. (If you used Option B of "Setting the Stage," refer back to that information now.) Have there been recent changes made to worship, your church constitution, or any aspect of your local congregation that the youth would remember? Why were these changes made?

Invite the youth to consider ways in which your church or denomination may need to be reformed. But be careful not to get into church bashing. You may want to invite a pastor or elder into the class with whom the youth would feel comfortable and who would be able to help youth understand why things are done in certain ways. Sure, there may be traditions that need to be changed, but perhaps the pastor, elder, or yourself could help the youth understand the original purpose behind those traditions so that youth may respect and not ridicule them, even in the midst of changing them.

Ask the youth how they might need to reform their own group traditions to better reflect their faith. Or invite them to consider (rather than simply dwelling on the ills of the past) a brand-new element they might bring to their youth classes, church worship, or some other aspect of church life that would reflect their faith. Be sure to act appropriately upon any suggestions that might be made. Close with prayer, asking God for insight into the proper ways to show our faith.

OPTION B
*Needed: worship materials, Bibles, hymnals or songbooks*
Invite the youth to close this session with a brief worship service of repentance and covenant. Begin by reading 2 Kings 23:1-3, in which Josiah makes a covenant of repentance and commitment. Invite the youth to shape their own covenant ceremony. They may write prayers, recite the *shema*, or choose a hymn or praise song to write together. Offer the worship preparation materials (prayer books, liturgy workbooks, etc.) and the hymnals or songbooks to the youth for their

planning. Provide assistance where needed, but be sure the youth design the brief worship by themselves. Close by sharing in your worship service.

**Things to Ponder**
Youth often find aspects of their worship life dissatisfying, with some legitimacy. Most of our congregations are set up in formats pleasing to folks of a different generation. However, little is to be gained by complaining. Rather, at all times we should maintain respect for history, tradition, and differing viewpoints. This does not, however, discount the value of raising new viewpoints and asking for a place at the table. In discussions of church reform, if you have them, challenge the youth to find respectful and appropriate ways to make their opinions heard by the church's decision makers. This will be a phenomenal lesson in leadership.

**Looking Ahead**
The next session includes several options for which you may want CDs of contemporary Christian music. If you do not have any, consider spending some time online or at a local Christian book store to find them. Generally, there are ways for you to listen to tracks for review before purchasing. Ask a salesclerk (or click on the bestseller listings) to see what is most popular with youth.

**Note**
1. Don't plan on anything too intense—a minute or two on the Lutheran Reformation, Vatican II, or any reform movements from your own denominational history will suffice.

# And the Scripture Says . . .

*Listen to the Scripture story and fill in as many answers below as you can when you hear them in the reading. (Not all the answers will be in the Scripture, though!)*

**1.** Josiah was how many years old when he started to reign? (Circle one.)   8   18   38   68

**2.** How old were you when you were in second grade? (Circle one.)   8   18   38   68

**3.** Josiah reigned for _____ years in Jerusalem.

**4.** Josiah's mom's name was (Circle one.):
Jennifer   Jocelyn   Jedidah   Joanie

**5.** Josiah (circle one)   did   did not do   what God wanted every day.

**6.** How old was Josiah when the story of the temple begins? (See verse 3.) _____

**7.** The high priest's name was (Circle one.):
Hezekiah   Nebuchadnezzar   James   Hilkiah

**8.** The secretary's name was (Circle one.):
Shaphan   Stephen   Samuel   Shelkiah

**9.** How much money from the Lord's house was going to be used to pay the workers? (Circle one.)
None of it   Half of it   All of it

**10.** What were the workers doing in the temple? (Circle one.)
Painting the bathrooms   Putting in new carpet
Repairing the wood and stone of the temple walls

**11.** Did Josiah trust the workers in the temple?   Yes   No

**12.** What was found in the temple? _____

**13.** Who found it? (Circle one.)
Josiah   Jedidah   Hilkiah   Shaphan

**14.** Who brought it to the king? (Circle one.)
Josiah   Jedidah   Hilkiah   Shaphan

**15.** Who read it aloud? (Circle one.)
Josiah   Jedidah   Hilkiah   Shaphan

**16.** What did Josiah do when he heard it? (Circle one.)
Cheer loudly   Call for his servants   Tear his clothes   Faint

**17.** "Great is the wrath of the Lᴏʀᴅ that is kindled against us, because our ancestors

_____ obey the words of this book" (verse 13).

**18.** The prophetess's name was (Circle one.):
Hilkiah     Haddad     Hannah     Huldah

**19.** According to the prophetess, God was going to do what to Jerusalem? (Circle one.)
Fix it up     Make it the capital city     Bring disaster to it

**20.** Why would God do this to Jerusalem? _____

**21.** But God also told the prophetess that Josiah would (Circle one.):
Be kidnapped     Die in peace     Reign for one hundred years

**22.** God would do this for Josiah because Josiah was (Circle one.):
Handsome     Repentant     Strong     David's heir

**Your Own Thoughts:**

What seems to be important to God about Josiah?

Why is Jerusalem going to be destroyed?

# Ready to Hear

*"Hear, O Israel: The LORD is our God, the LORD alone. You shall love the LORD your God with all your heart, and with all your soul, and with all your might."—Deuteronomy 6:4-5*

The quotation above is referred to in Hebrew simply as the *shema. Shema* is the Hebrew word for "hear." The *shema* is possibly one of the most significant pairs of verses in the Hebrew Scriptures, for it governs the entire life of a Jewish person. Everything they do, every day, is to reflect their love of the Lord.

The *shema* occurs early in what is called the Deuteronomic history. This history is the one put together by a historian, or group of historians, who wanted to show how God acted through history in the lives of the chosen people. The story from 2 Kings that we are looking at in this session is also part of the Deuteronomic history. For this historian, or group of historians, *hearing* the word of the Lord implies *obedience* to the word of the Lord. Hearing is doing. All of Israel's history, for this historian, is judged by how well the people lived out the *shema.*

You may remember Jesus using this same idea. Read Matthew 13:1-23 for a great example of this. For Jesus, having "ears to hear" also implies understanding and obeying.

Josiah was ready to hear the word of the Lord. Hearing it helped him realize how far his people were from following it. He must already have been obedient himself to be able to understand this.

Consider now, privately, whether you truly have ears to hear. Think about the words of the *shema.* How well have you done in living those words in your life? Are there ways you could do better? Are you ready to try to do better or not? Why or why not? Write below (and use the back of this page if you need to) your thoughts about these questions and any other insights you might have. (No one else will see this. It's just between you and God!)

# 11. A New Covenant

*Bible Story: Jeremiah 31:31-34*

Lisa and Chris Holliday

## A Story behind the Story

The Hebrew people have passed generations since their covenant with God at the base of Mount Sinai. The giving of the Ten Commandments has become a distant memory. As they intermingle more and more with the surrounding nations, they assimilate the worship of other gods into their own worship, drifting further and further away from their original covenantal relationship with God. When the kingdom splits apart into the lands of Israel and Judah, their relationship with God as God's chosen people is shaky at best. The northern kingdom of Israel is conquered by the Assyrians, the Israelites sent into exile. The southern kingdom of Judah negotiates an insecure peace with Assyria, becoming a tributary nation but maintaining its own monarchy.

It is during this time (more than 650 years since the Mount Sinai covenant) that God calls Jeremiah to be a prophet in the southern kingdom of Judah. Josiah is king of Judah, and during his reign, he asserts Judah's independence from Assyria. In what Bible scholars typically refer to as "the reform of Josiah," this faithful king starts leading the people back toward God. Jeremiah, however, still sees too much disobedience to God, and he preaches of the doom that will come. After a scroll of God's laws is found in the temple, King Josiah and the people promise God that they will obey, and a more radical reform is begun. About twelve years later, Judah is conquered by the Egyptians and King Josiah is killed.

After Josiah's death, we find Jeremiah again preaching doom. He encourages the people to surrender to the Babylonians and to accept this defeat as their inevitable punishment from God. Eventually, Judah is seized by King Nebuchadnezzar and the Babylonians. Ultimately, Jerusalem is destroyed and many Judeans are deported to Babylon (the Exile).

After the destruction of Jerusalem and the Exile, Jeremiah's message changes to one of consolation, hope, return, and restoration. In this session's Scripture we find Jeremiah writing to the exiles about a new covenant between God and people—one that is unconditional and unfailing; one that is based on forgiveness, redemptive love, grace, and a more personal relationship; one from which a restored community of God will arise. Some consider this passage a foreshadowing of the new covenant realized through Christ.

## Enter the Story

The Book of Jeremiah is not chronologically arranged, but most scholars believe chapters 30 and 31 are among the last letters Jeremiah wrote to the exiles in Babylon. These letters are usually called "the Book of Consolation." Take time to read and reflect on these two chapters. Also read 32:37-41, which further explains the new covenant.

Consider those parts of your own life that need consolation. What are you afraid of? What yoke is upon

## POSSIBLE YOUTH CONTACT POINTS

- What people or issues oppress and hurt me?
- Will God punish me when I do wrong?
- Is God's love really unconditional?
- Am I keeping my covenants to God and to others?
- How can I open my heart to God?
- How could God forgive me after what I've done?

## YOU MAY NEED

- Bibles
- newsprint and markers
- Bible study resources
- writing utensils
- blank paper (8½" x 11" and some larger than that)
- colored pencils, thin markers, or crayons
- foam ball
- CD or tape player
- contemporary Christian CDs or tapes
- "Of Course, I Know Ya!" handouts
- candle
- matches or lighter
- modeling clay
- large paper clips
- newspapers and magazines
- poster board
- glue
- scissors (one per person)
- "What's New?" handouts
- letter cereal or letter pretzels
- closing song
- strips of paper
- container in which to safely burn paper

you? How does the word *restoration* apply to your life right now? What covenants have you broken? What covenants have you kept? What has God written on your heart? What does knowing God mean to you? What comforts you about the new covenant? Spend some time reflecting on the amazing grace of God and the forgiveness God offers you and everyone. Do you feel forgiven? Do you trust in God's grace?

### Setting the Stage (5–10 minutes)
OPTION A
*Needed: foam ball, CD or tape player, upbeat contemporary Christian CD or tape*
Ask the youth to form a circle. Say: *This game will help us see how well we know each other. As the group quickly throws the foam ball back and forth across the circle, I will play some music. When the music stops, whoever has the ball must go to the middle of the circle. Then the group has one minute to say what we know about the person. Some examples of things we could mention about the person are:* [list some ideas from the "Of Course, I Know Ya!" handout]. Explain that after the minute is up, the person in the middle should politely correct any misinformation and return to the circle. Then start the process again. Each person should go only once. If a person who has been in the middle ends up with the ball when the music stops, he or she must select someone who has not gone to go into the middle.

Help the youth stay considerate with their comments, being careful not to say anything embarrassing or

mean-spirited. If you have any visitors whom the youth do not know, you could give those visitors the option of passing or of telling the group a little about themselves when it is their turn. Another option is to have the friend whom the visitor came with go into the middle with the visitor and introduce her or him to the group. End by briefly reflecting with the group on how well they know each other.

OPTION B
*Needed: writing utensils, "Of Course, I Know Ya!" handouts*
Ask each youth to pair up with someone who knows them really well. Tell them that this exercise will help them find out how well they know each other. Give each person a copy of the handout "Of Course, I Know Ya!," and a writing utensil. Help the youth notice that the handout questions in section A are all about their partner. Ask each youth to complete section A without help from their partner and without letting their partner see what their responses are. Ask them to wait to work on section B.

Next, ask each pair to share their responses with each other, to correct any incorrect responses, and to complete section B together. When the pairs are finished, bring the group back together and lead a brief discussion based on the questions in section B.

### Telling the Story (5–10 minutes)
OPTION A
*Needed: candle, matches or lighter, Bible*
Light a candle and turn off the lights. Tell the youth that God and

humanity have been making covenants for a long time and that our Scripture for today introduces a new covenant between God and the people of Israel and Judah. Summarize the information in "A Story behind the Story" to give the youth the background of the covenant history of the Hebrew people.

Ask everyone to close their eyes and listen closely to the Scripture. Tell them that you will read it twice with a time of silence after each reading. Invite them to hang on to a word or phrase that seems to speak to them during the first reading, and ask them to reflect on what that word or phrase says to them during the time of silence. During the second reading, ask them to do the same thing and to see if a different word or phrase pops out at them. Ask the youth to listen to what God might say to them through this Scripture.

OPTION B
*Needed: Bible, modeling clay, large paper clips*
Tell the youth that God and humanity have been making covenants for a long time and that our Scripture for today introduces a new covenant between God and the people of Israel and Judah. Summarize the information in "A Story behind the Story" to give the youth the background of the covenant history of the Hebrew people.

Give each youth a piece of clay and a large paper clip. Ask each youth to straighten out the paper clip so that he or she can use it to write in the clay. Tell the youth that you are going to read the Scripture passage three times with a period of silence following each reading.

Before you begin reading, invite each person to do the following: (1) sit quietly and listen carefully to the first reading; (2) mold the clay into the shape of a heart during the second reading; (3) write a word or a phrase on the clay heart using the paper clip during the third reading. Tell everyone that the word or phrase should be one that stands out to them and that it can come from the Scripture or from their own reflections on the passage.

**Reacting to the Story (15–20 minutes)**
OPTION A
*Needed: newsprint and markers, Bibles, possibly clay hearts*
If you used option A above, invite each student to share the words or phrases that stood out to them and their general reflections on the passage. If you used option B, have the students show their clay hearts and ask them to share their words and phrases and general reflections.

List all the words and phrases and key comments on newsprint. If a word or phrase is said more than once, keep a tally of how many people mentioned it. Affirm the youth for their reflection efforts and their insight.

Ask the group to get out their Bibles and turn to Jeremiah 31:31-34. Ask:
■ What does "I will put my law within them, and I will write it on their hearts" (verse 33) say to you?
■ How can someone "know" the Lord better?
■ What does it mean to be God's people?
■ Who does the Scripture say will know God? What does that mean to you?

■ Do you think that God really forgives and forgets?

OPTION B
*Needed: Bibles, newsprint and markers*
Split the youth into small groups and have each group elect a reporter. Give each group newsprint and markers. Have the youth write their names on the top left corner of their group's piece of newsprint.

Invite the youth to pretend that they are in exile in Babylon. They have just received this letter from Jeremiah containing the words from 31:31-34. Now have each small group respond by writing a letter back to Jeremiah. The letter should contain all their questions and reflections on the passage. Offer a sample question in case groups get stuck. For example, you could ask any of the following:
■ When are the days of this new covenant coming?
■ What is the old covenant Jeremiah is referring to?
■ What does it mean to be God's people?
■ How can we "know" God, and who else will know God?
■ Will God really forgive and forget all our sins?

After the youth have had time to come up with questions and reflections, gather the group back together. Have a person from each group hold up the newsprint while the reporter shares the group's questions and comments. Tell the groups that they will get a chance to find some of the answers to their questions later in the session. Collect their newsprints to use in "Exploring the Story," Option B.

## Connecting to the Story (15–20 minutes)
OPTION A
*Needed: colored pencils, thin markers, or crayons, large blank paper, CD or tape player, contemporary Christian CD or tape*
In our Scripture passage for this lesson, God speaks through the prophet Jeremiah. One of God's main desires is that we all "know" God. The purpose of this exercise is to help the youth discover how they know God and how God is involved in their life journey.

Give each youth a large blank piece of paper and make available colored pencils, thin markers, or crayons. Explain to the students that they are to draw a time line of their life with God so far. Ask them to consider major events as well as more routine times. They are to consider any interaction with God they've had and to represent as much of it as possible on this time line. When did they begin to know God, and how has that understanding changed over the years? What covenants have they made with God? When has God offered them forgiveness?

Invite everyone to use pictures, words, symbols, or markings of any kind to create this project. Instruct youth to fold the paper or to list events and pictures right to left, top to bottom, etc. Encourage them to do whatever seems to represent their time of knowing God best. Play some contemporary Christian music while they work on this section.

After everyone has completed their time lines, ask for volunteers to share their time lines with the group.

OPTION B

*Needed: newspapers, magazines, poster board, glue, scissors, markers, newsprint, CD or tape player, contemporary Christian CD or tape*

Divide the youth into small groups. Read Jeremiah 31:33. Ask the youth: *What does this verse say that God desires?* List their responses on newsprint.

Make sure each small group has a piece of poster board, some newspapers and magazines, glue, scissors, and a marker. Instruct each group to draw an outline of a large heart on their piece of poster board. Have the youth show how people of today are being God's people by filling the heart with pictures and words from the magazines and newspapers. How are the ways of God written on our world's "heart"? You could play some contemporary Christian music during this section.

When all the groups are finished, have each group share their heart posters with the large group.

## Exploring the Story
### (15–20 minutes)

OPTION A

*Needed: Bibles, writing utensils, "What's New?" handouts, newsprint and markers*

Divide the youth into small groups and ask them to take their Bibles and writing utensils with them. Give each youth a "What's New?" handout. Invite them to read the Scriptures listed on the top of the handout, and have each small group complete their handouts together.

Before the session or while the groups work on their task, transfer the handout headings to newsprint. Then walk around and observe the youth, lending assistance if it's needed. Once everyone is finished, gather the large group and have each person share one similarity or difference between the covenants that he or she discovered. As you write their responses on newsprint, invite each youth to check off the similarities and differences they recorded and to add to their handouts any additional ones. Once you have heard from everyone, continue going around the group until you have listed all the similarities and differences found.

Take some time to reflect with the youth on their findings.

■ What's new about this new covenant?

■ What do you like or dislike about it?

■ Is the image of God different in the old covenant as compared to the new? If so, how?

OPTION B

*(This option follows Option B of "Reacting to the Story.")*

*Needed: newsprints from Option B of "Reacting to the Story," paper, pencils, Bible study resources*

Ask the small groups from "Reacting to the Story," Option B, to gather again. Give back to each group its newsprint of initial questions and comments. Ask the groups to add any new questions or comments to their list. Make available commentaries, study Bibles, Bible dictionaries, concordances, and different translations of the Bible, or use computers and Bible study software if you have them available to you.

Ask each group to research their questions and comments. Hopefully, this process will help the youth gain a greater understanding of God, the Scripture, and some of the people and events involved. Have each small group elect a new reporter who will take notes of the group's findings. After allowing adequate time for research, gather the large group together and have each reporter share the group's findings.

**Living the Story
(5–10 minutes)**
OPTION A
*Needed: Bibles, newsprint and markers, letter cereal or letter pretzels, candle, matches or lighter, closing song*
Talk with the class about God's desire to "put my law within them, and . . . write it on their hearts" (verse 33). Ask the youth to brainstorm places where God's law has been written previously, and list their responses on newsprint. (Examples can be found in Exodus 24:12, Deuteronomy 6:8-9, and 2 Kings 22:8.)
    Ask the youth:
■ What's different about the law being within people as compared to the law being written in other places?
■ Does the new covenant change the relationship between God and God's people? If so, how?
    Invite each student to think of a word or phrase that sums up the laws and ways of God for them (Matthew 22:34-40 may be helpful). Ask each student to use the letter cereal or letter pretzels to spell

out that word or phrase. Have the group sit in a circle with their letters in hand. Turn off the lights and put a lit candle in the center of the circle. Invite the youth to quietly reflect on God's new covenant and their word or phrase.
    After a few minutes, say: *Let us put God's law within us, and let us keep it in our hearts from this day forward.* Invite the youth to eat their word or phrase at this time. Once the group eats, have everyone stand, hold hands, and sing something like the first verse of "Blest Be the Tie That Binds." End by pronouncing a short benediction, such as *Go forth, knowing that the word of the Lord is within you. Go in peace. Amen.*

OPTION B
*Needed: strips of paper, writing utensils, contemporary Christian CD or tape, CD or tape player, container for safely burning paper, matches or lighter, closing song*
Remind the youth that the new covenant involves God's willingness to forgive and forget their sins (verse 34). Give each youth a strip of paper and a pencil and ask them to find a quiet place away from the others. Invite them to list their sins on the paper and to silently pray to God for forgiveness. Play some meditative music during this time.
    After they finish, lead the group to a place where you can have fire safely. Burn the slips of paper one at a time or as a group. After this process, sing a song such as "Amazing Grace" or "Awesome God." End by pronouncing a benediction, such as *Go forth, knowing that*

*your sins are forgiven. Go in peace. Amen.*

## Things to Ponder

The youth in your class might be struggling with issues such as how to know God, how to let God into their hearts and lives, broken covenants, trust, guilt, and forgiveness. Pray for each person in your group this week, and journal or think about any specific challenges the youth are facing. Follow up with individual youth as appropriate.

Also take time to consider how the session went. Which activities worked best and why? What do you wish you would have done differently to help the youth get the most out of your time together?

## Looking Ahead

You may need to collect worship bulletins from past church services. Your church secretary should be a good resource for this. In addition, you may need to find stalks of wheat. If you don't have any farmers in your congregation, dried wheat or wheatlike grasses should be available at craft stores or florist shops inexpensively.

# Of Course, I Know Ya!

## Section A

**1.** What is your partner's full name?

**2.** What school does he or she attend?

**3.** What is your partner's favorite subject in school?

**4.** What are her or his favorite foods?

**5.** What is your partner's favorite type of music, and who is his or her favorite musical artist(s)?

**6.** Who is your partner's favorite actor?

**7.** What is her or his favorite TV show and movie?

**8.** What is your partner's date of birth, including the year?

**9.** Does she or he have a pet? What kind, and what's the pet's name?

**10.** Who are the significant family members in his or her life?

**11.** What are your partner's interests and hobbies?

**12.** What are her or his best personality traits?

**13.** How long have you known your partner?

## Section B

**1.** Do you know your partner as well as you thought you did?

**2.** Circle the number that best represents how well you know your partner.

Not very well                                  Extremely well

1     2     3     4     5     6     7     8     9     10

**3.** Did you find out anything about him or her that surprised you? If so, what?

**4.** How do you really get to know someone?

## What's New?

*Read these highlights of the old covenant between God and Israel:*

**Exodus 6:6-9, 20:1-21, and 24:1-8**

*Read these highlights of the new covenant:*

**Jeremiah 24:1-10, 31:31-34, and 32:37-41**

*Compare and contrast the two covenants.*

What's the same?

What's different?

So, what's *new* about the new covenant?

# 12. The Sabbath

*Bible Story: Mark 2:23-28*

Sandra DeMott Hasenauer

## A Story behind the Story

The original audience of the Gospel of Mark was trying to figure out its relationship to the Jewish tradition from which it arose. Just how much of the original Hebrew law applied to this new community with its focus on Jesus Christ? How should Christians apply the words of the law to the spirit of discipleship? The questions raised in the Scripture story for this session are these types of questions.

It would be far too easy to attribute the challenge offered by the Pharisees to blind legalism. The fact is that the question they asked does not necessarily have a clear-cut answer even in Jewish tradition. There was debate about exactly what constitutes "work," and what room is allowed for human need, in the sabbath traditions of the time. However, the question-and-answer exchange between Jesus and the Pharisees can certainly be understood in light of the early Christians trying to figure out for themselves how to understand sabbath as a part of their faith.

Is there restrictive legalism evident in the Pharisees' question? Certainly. Is there restrictive legalism in our own attitudes and traditions surrounding sabbath observance? Or—and perhaps worse—is there a new laxity that buys into the secular, self-absorbed culture based on the freedom from regulation we're assuming Jesus is bringing us? Perhaps. It is just that "perhaps" that drives us to study our own attitudes and understandings of a sabbath rest and its relationship to our faith.

Jesus tells the Pharisees that the "sabbath was made for humankind, not humankind for the sabbath" (verse 27). The sabbath is a gift, a day when we can rest in the presence and care of God, a time when we can renew ourselves and refocus on our relationship with our Creator. Unfortunately, our sabbath day has become secularized to the point where it alternates between being a selfish exercise in luxury, focusing only on our own needs and not on our relationship with God, and being a busy day filled with sports, extra work, and chores around the house—equally without focusing on our relationship with God. Surely, neither of those is what Jesus intended. Remember, Jesus states his own authority over the sabbath. Our sabbath rest is governed by Christ, not by rules and not by our own needs.

## Enter the Story

Consider your own sabbath practices. These may or may not actually involve your thoughts of church attendance. All too frequently, those of us involved in church leadership begin to view church as a "job" rather than part of a day of rest. We need to sort these feelings out, lest we suffer from burnout and end up losing our sense of ministry.

When was a time you truly felt you were experiencing sabbath?

Perhaps it was on a church retreat or at a denominational conference. Perhaps it was during a sick day at home when you found unexpected time to use in prayer or spiritual practices. Perhaps it was in the midst of a vacation, when you felt God's presence in nature. We are gifted with sabbath in many ways and sometimes in surprising places. However, as much as God likes to surprise us, we also are called to set aside regular times in our lives to focus on God's presence.

Review your own sabbath practices; are they working for you? Read Mark 2:23-28, and then have some conversation with God about your sabbath. Maybe some changes need to be made in your sabbath observances.

## Setting the Stage (5–10 minutes)

OPTION A

*Needed: church bulletins from past worship services, newsprint and marker or chalkboard and chalk, newsprint or chalkboard prepared with the definition of "sabbath"*

After youth enter, spend a few moments checking in with them about their experiences during the time that has elapsed since your last session together. What were their high points and low points? Does anyone have anything coming up that they want to share (such as exams, elections, vacation plans, driver's tests, etc.)? Open with a few moments of prayer, including prayers for any youth who raised particular events or issues.

After the prayer, give each youth a copy of an old church bulletin. Ask: *How do we celebrate the*

*Lord's day in our church?* List some of the things they mention on blank newsprint or chalkboard. If your bulletin lists calendar items or postings of meetings, etc., encourage the youth to look beyond the typical morning worship outline. (This would also include Christian education classes.)

After you've listed several things, ask: *Are Sundays [or Saturdays— whichever day your tradition considers its "sabbath"] restful for you? Why or why not?* Show the youth the definition of *sabbath* you've written out. Ask the youth:

■ Does anything on this bulletin fit with this definition? Why or why not?

■ Do you have a time in your week that matches this definition?

Inform the youth that today's Scripture story is all about sabbath.

OPTION B

Ask the youth to think of an example of a time when they met a friend whom they hadn't seen for a long time. Has anyone ever had that experience? If so, what did they do to renew the acquaintance?

If no one has had this sort of experience, ask them:

■ How do you become friends with someone?

■ What marks a close friendship?

Chances are, "spending time together" will develop as an overarching theme.

Invite the youth to consider how their relationship with God might be like a friendship. Do they have a chance to become close if they never spend time with God? Offer youth this definition of *sabbath*: "a chance to spend some time with God." If

## POSSIBLE YOUTH CONTACT POINTS

■ **What does *sabbath* mean?**
■ **How do I make a sabbath into Jesus' day?**
■ **How do I worship God?**

## YOU MAY NEED

■ **church bulletins from past worship services (for two different potential options)**
■ **newsprint and marker *or* chalkboard and chalk**
■ **newsprint or chalkboard prepared with this definition of *sabbath*: "a day of rest and worship, a day of relationship with God"**
■ **Bibles**
■ **props and costumes (optional)**
■ **stalks of wheat (or any dried grass that looks like wheat, available at floral or craft stores and at some grocery stores with a floral department)**
■ **"Keepin' It Holy" handouts**
■ **writing utensils**
■ **Bible concordances[1]**
■ **paper**
■ **Bible study helps, such as commentaries on Mark, concordances, atlases, Bible encyclopedias, and Bible dictionaries.**
■ **construction paper "stalk" (see Option A, "Living the Story")**
■ **construction paper**
■ **"Grain of Wheat" handouts (2–3 copies)**
■ **scissors**
■ **markers**
■ **masking tape**

this definition is accurate, can any of them name regular times in their lives that might be considered sabbath? Let them know that today's Scripture story is about sabbath.

## Telling the Story (5–10 minutes)

OPTION A

*Needed: Bibles, props and costumes (optional)*

Invite volunteers to role-play the different characters of the Scripture: Jesus, the Pharisees, the disciples. You may choose to involve only three youth (with one Pharisee and one disciple), or you can involve everyone in the class by expanding the number of Pharisees and disciples. You will also need someone to serve as narrator. Have the volunteers read the Scripture in their parts while doing their best to act out the scene. Offer such props or costumes as you may have readily available.

Since it is a short Scripture, consider having youth trade parts and reading through it again, encouraging these new actors to find some different tone of voice to use for reading their lines. This will help them see how the Scripture may be looked at differently, considering different ways the sayings may be understood.

Consider also having the youth imagine how this same Scripture might look if it were brought into their own community and time: What might the disciples be doing rather than plucking wheat? Who would be the Pharisees? If you have time, role-play the biblical story first in its original biblical setting and then do it a second time, with

the youth role-playing this current-day setting. Afterward, ask if the current-day setting helped them to understand the Scripture differently. If so, how?

OPTION B

*Needed: stalks of wheat, Bibles*

Give each youth a stalk of wheat and encourage them to feel it, look at its details, and smell it. Invite them to hold on to these stalks while reading the Scripture story. You may choose to find volunteers to read the story in whatever manner your group is most comfortable with: all reading in round-robin fashion, one or two volunteers reading a collection of verses, or one good reader giving inflection to the entire passage. Each time the word *sabbath* is read, have the youth raise up their stalks of wheat and shake them around, calling out "Sabbath!" at the top of their lungs. They may have to be somewhat gentle in shaking the stalks of wheat lest the stalks snap.

## Reacting to the Story (10–15 minutes)

OPTION A

*Needed: newsprint and marker or chalkboard and chalk, Bibles*

Take a few moments and invite the youth to raise any questions they may have about the passage, now that they've read it. An obvious first one might be *What's "sabbath"?* Do not attempt to answer any of the questions at this point, or if the group offers answers, list those next to the questions for future reference. Encourage them to refer to the story in their Bibles, rereading it verse by verse and asking after each verse, *Any questions about this part? Any words you don't understand or people you don't know?* For example, they should probably question the story about David mentioned in verse 25; it's not familiar to most youth groups.

After you've got a fairly lengthy list, ask your learners if they feel that finding answers to any of those questions might help them understand the passage better. Not all of the questions will seem as important to the youth as others. Have them go through the list and put asterisks next to the questions that they feel might actually have an impact upon their understanding of this passage. The group need not be unanimous; if there is a question that only one person feels is important, go ahead and put an asterisk next to it. Save this list for use in "Exploring the Story," Option B.

OPTION B
*Needed: Bibles, newsprint and marker or chalkboard and chalk*
Invite the youth to have a discussion about the concept of sabbath. This will, of course, be preliminary to them having done any actual study on it later in the session. However, their church tradition may have given them certain understandings of sabbath or they may simply have some feeling about it based on the Scripture itself. Ask such questions as these to spur discussion:
■ What is sabbath?
■ Who created the sabbath?
■ Do you know where it comes from?
■ Is sabbath important? Why or why not?

■ What kinds of things should be done to observe a sabbath? (You might also ask if they are familiar with the term *sabbatical* and how that might be related to the sabbath.)

Tell the group that they will have an opportunity to explore the concept of sabbath throughout the session.

## Connecting to the Story (10–15 minutes)
OPTION A
*Needed: "Keepin' It Holy" handouts, writing utensils, Bibles*
Give each youth a copy of the "Keepin' It Holy" handouts and a writing utensil. Invite them to keep their Bibles open to Mark 2:23-28. Review any discussions you may have already had during the session about the concept of sabbath. Read for them Exodus 20:8. Invite the class to consider how they might go about keeping the sabbath holy: *If Sunday [or Saturday] is considered the "sabbath" in our church, how would we go about keeping it holy?*

Directing the youth's attention to the handout, tell them to fill in the grains of wheat with ideas about how they would keep the sabbath holy. They may use a word or a phrase in each grain, and they should be as specific as possible. Encourage them to fill in all the grains of wheat to the best of their ability. This will challenge them to think more broadly than the obvious "go to church" and "pray."

As they are beginning their work, invite them to consider their schedule, their interactions with family members, their relationship with God. What might they do to make sure this particular day is kept holy and focused on God? Remind them to reread Jesus' statements in Mark 2:27-28 as they do their work. How will their ideas reflect these statements?

After they've had some time to work on the handouts themselves, bring them back into the whole class (or if you've got a large class, into groups of three or four) to share their ideas with each other.

OPTION B
*Needed: church bulletins of past worship services*
Make sure each youth has access to a church bulletin (either one per person or two people sharing a bulletin). Invite the class to review the church bulletins for hints of sabbath. In other words, are there portions of worship that could be considered truly sabbath? Why or why not? Keep in mind that the youth may have different opinions on this. While listening to the choir anthem may be a spiritual experience for one youth, another one may hate the music so much that it is a deterrent to sabbath. The pastoral prayer may or may not be an experience of sabbath for the youth, and the same may go for the sermon. Again, the definition of *sabbath* may come into question; encourage discussion and continued development of their understanding of sabbath.

## Exploring the Story (10–15 minutes)
OPTION A
*Needed: Bible concordances (or photocopies from a concordance),*

*Bibles, paper, writing utensils, newsprint and markers or chalkboard and chalk*
Not surprisingly, a fair amount of space is given to the sabbath and its regulations in the Old Testament. Break the class into groups of three or four. (Smaller classes can work as a full class or in pairs.) Make sure each small group has access to a concordance (or to photocopied pages of one), writing utensils, and Bibles.

Invite the groups to look up the references to "sabbath" that are listed in the concordance and find those passages in their Bibles. Most concordances will give a sentence fragment with the Scripture citation. If they see several sentence fragments that look similar, they might consider looking up only one or two of those citations. They should take particular care to look at the original sabbath commandment in the Ten Commandments (Exodus 20). Have them list the different things said about sabbath on their paper, dividing it into two columns. In the first column, they should list things they find out about the *purpose* of the sabbath; in the second, they should list those things that are specific to the *observance* of the sabbath.

Once they have done some work, bring the class together and share their findings as a large group. What have they discovered about the sabbath?

Finally, have them compare these findings with Jesus' statement in Mark 2:27-28. What is Jesus saying about the Sabbath? What would

Jesus have us consider in our Sabbath observances?

OPTION B
*Needed: Bible study helps, list of questions from Option A of "Reacting to the Story," Bibles, paper, writing utensils*
Invite the class to review the list of questions they created in Option A of "Reacting to the Story." In smaller groups (pairs or individuals, if they choose), invite the youth to choose a question they would like to study. Make appropriate Bible study helps available to the youth, and be available to assist. After the youth have had some time to explore their questions (and they may or may not find answers), invite them to share their questions and findings with the rest of the class. For those groups unable to find answers, encourage them to consider their own responses to the questions. Debate these points as a class, reminding the youth that Christians have been debating questions like these for centuries.

**Living the Story (5–10 minutes)**
OPTION A
*Needed: construction paper "stalk," construction paper, "Grain of Wheat" handouts, scissors, markers, masking tape*
Ahead of time, make a large construction paper "stalk" (see the drawing on the handouts for a possible design) out of wheat-colored construction paper, and write the word *sabbath* in large letters on the stalk. Tape the stalk to the wall in a place that will have enough room for additions to it.

At the end of your class session, make construction paper and scissors available to the youth. Invite them to cut out one or two large "grains of wheat," as shown on the "Grain of Wheat" handouts. Consider making two or three copies of the handout available to the youth to use as a template if they're not confident in their own design abilities.

After each youth has one or two construction paper grains cut out, make sure each person has a marker. Invite the youth to consider all of the discussions you've had together during the session about keeping sabbath holy. Ask each youth to think of one or two things they are ready to commit to doing so as to observe a sabbath the way God would want them to do. They should then write these things, one per grain. Encourage each youth to use at least one grain.

After everyone (including yourself) has a paper grain prepared, close your session with a time of prayer together, thanking God for the gift of sabbath and asking God's help in attending to your sabbath observances. At an appropriate time during the prayer, invite the youth to come forward, say what is written on their grain, and place their grains along the edges of the paper stalk you prepared earlier, creating one large shaft of wheat on your wall. After each person tapes up his or her grain, have the group respond with *God, thank you for sabbath.* When all are done, close the prayer.

OPTION B

*Needed: Bibles, newsprint, markers*

Invite the youth to plan a weekend sabbath retreat for the class. Reviewing your discussions and findings during the session, ask the youth to consider what a sabbath retreat might include. What would not be included? What might the rhythm of the weekend involve? Be sure to follow through on scheduling the retreat! Close your session in prayer, thanking God for the gift of sabbath.

## Things to Ponder

Good sabbath observance is something everyone needs to think about, both youth and adults. Particularly in a world that values busyness and overinvolvement, times to refresh and renew our relationship with God need to be intentionally planned and kept as a high priority, lest they get lost in the shuffle. Plan to include times of sabbath for your youth throughout the year, if you are in a position to do so. An afternoon of quiet reflection during a retreat, a prayer service, or an actual sabbath retreat may not sound exciting to the youth to begin with, but they will welcome it when it comes.

## Looking Ahead

For the next session, you may need to gather resources that give your denomination's view of the Lord's Supper (the Eucharist, or Communion). Also, you may have the opportunity to invite your pastor into the classroom to help the youth discuss the same topic. Be sure to contact the pastor well in advance to get on her or his schedule.

## Note

1. If you have only one concordance available, make copies of the pages listing the word *sabbath*. You will need several identical sets of copies—one per small group. (This will not be copyright infringement as long as they are for teaching purposes in a nonprofit institution, with a one-time use intent. You should include a copy of the title page, or verbally inform the youth from which book the copies came, and then destroy any copies following the class.)

Keepin' It Holy

Sabbath

Grain of Wheat

# 13. Road to Emmaus

*Bible Story: Luke 24:13-35*

Sandra DeMott Hasenauer

## A Story behind the Story

Entertaining angels unawares—this is a theme that has traveled throughout our history of faith, beginning in the stories of the Old Testament. (Remember Abraham and the three visitors right before the Sodom incident?) But this week's story, about Jesus on the road to Emmaus, is the ultimate "angels unawares" story, for here is no angel at all but rather our Lord Jesus Christ walking next to the unsuspecting disciples.

In fact, the disciples are "kept from recognizing him" (verse 16) to begin with. Their failure to know him isn't stupidity at all but rather some sort of divine plan. Perhaps this is a twist on the statement Jesus makes to Thomas: "Have you believed because you have seen me? Blessed are those who have not seen and yet have come to believe" (John 20:29). These disciples have not seen, yet they eagerly share with this stranger the story of their Christ.

However, their story isn't exactly right. The story they share describes Jesus as a prophet and expresses sadness at his crucifixion. They declare an unrealized hope in the redemption of Israel and, in this, their lack of belief is revealed. Despite the evidence of the empty tomb and the word of the women witnesses of the risen Savior, they still walk in sadness and uncertainty. But the stranger's very presence, walking on the road beside them, lets the reader in on the joyful irony of the story: the Resurrection has occurred. Redemption is present, if only they could see it.

Revelation is necessary to see Christ's presence. Hearing the stories is a wonderful start. But as we see in the interaction on the road to Emmaus, the stories themselves are not enough to make someone believe. Jesus reveals himself in the breaking of the bread. Sitting at table with the disciples, he takes bread, blesses it, breaks it, and gives it to them—and their eyes are opened. These four words of the Eucharist, *take, bless, break,* and *give,* represent the actions that reveal Christ to the disciples.

Each time you share in the Lord's Supper with your congregation, is Christ revealed to you in the breaking of the bread? Each time you share table fellowship with your family, with friends, or with strangers, is Christ revealed in the breaking of the bread? Jesus reveals himself to us in these everyday events—the necessary ritual of eating, important to our very survival—and blessed indeed are those who see.

## Enter the Story

If you have the opportunity, take a good, long walk before sitting down to read this story. The Scripture tells us that the disciples were on a journey of about seven miles—but you don't have to walk *that* far! As you're walking, imagine someone appearing beside you and asking questions. Be honest—how would you feel? Try to put yourself in the shoes of these disciples before you sit down to read the story from Scripture.

- How would I recognize Jesus?
- Would I be willing to tell the story of Jesus to a stranger?
- Would I ever eat at the same table with a stranger?
- Have I ever invited Jesus to be a part of my life?

## YOU MAY NEED

- predetermined path through the church or outside
- Bibles
- unleavened bread, such as matzo crackers or pita bread
- napkins
- newsprint and markers *or* chalkboard and chalk
- writing paper
- writing utensils
- construction paper
- crayons
- newsprint and markers *or* chalkboard and chalk, with sections written out as described in Option B of "Reacting to the Story" (optional)
- scissors
- devotional story (optional)
- "Eating with Jesus" handouts
- snacks
- church liturgy for the Eucharist (Communion, or Lord's Supper)
- pastor (optional)
- "An Invitation" handouts
- CD player and CD (optional)
- worship planning resources, such as prayer books, hymnals, liturgy workbooks, etc.

Pray before reading, and make sure you've got some time to reflect on these verses. What story of Jesus would you tell someone who asked? How would you recognize Jesus? Do you feel that Christ is revealed to you in your church's observance of the Eucharist (or the Lord's Supper)?

## Setting the Stage (5–10 minutes)

OPTION A

Welcome the youth and spend a few moments checking in with them on the events of their lives since you were last together. Encourage them to share stories with you—the stories of these events and how they made them feel. After you've spent a few moments like this, ask whether the youth have ever been asked to share a story with a stranger of something meaningful in their lives. Perhaps something like that happened at a youth conference or a school event. How did it make them feel?

Ask the youth to consider how much storytelling is a part of their church life. Do they deal with stories in worship? How? In religious education classes? During church fellowship events? What kinds of stories? What functions do these stories have?

Let the group know that, in the early Christian church, the main activities of worship were sharing the stories of Jesus and other Scriptures, reflecting on these stories, and "breaking bread" (in other words, sharing a meal) together. "Where two or three are gathered in my name, I am there among them," Jesus promised (Matthew 18:20). We have all the elements of worship here in the story we're looking at today.

OPTION B

Welcome the youth and spend some time checking in with them as described above. However, in this option, ask the youth to think about whether anything surprising happened to them during the time you were apart since the last session. Was it a good surprise or a not-so-good surprise? Invite the youth to think about any time in their lives when they experienced a good surprise. What was the surprise? Why was it a surprise? How did it make them feel? (You may want to begin with a brief story of your own to help youth make connections with their own stories.)

If no one has already shared this kind of a story, ask the class to consider:

- Was there ever a time when you were prepared for bad news but received good news instead?
- Was there ever a time when you found out that what you thought was terrible was actually really good?

Invite them to describe the event and how it made them feel.

After a few minutes of sharing these kinds of stories, inform the youth that today's Scripture story is all about the disciples receiving a wonderful surprise.

## Telling the Story (5–10 minutes)

OPTION A

*Needed: a predetermined path through the church or outside, Bibles*

As other stories in these sessions have been, this is a "moving" story. Since the disciples are walking throughout most of the story, consider taking the class on a walk through or outside of the church building while they are reading the story. If you have a very large class, consider breaking them into two or three smaller groups (each with an adult leader), so that they can hear the story better. Each group may choose to take a different path.

Share the reading among the group in some way, and follow the Scripture in terms of when to stop. For example, you may want to stop at some point near, but not back to, your classroom for the scene in the house. Read the entire indoor section of the story in that location and then continue your walk back to the classroom as the disciples return to Jerusalem to tell the other disciples about their experience.

Once you've returned to the classroom and finished the story, ask the youth to quickly summarize the events of the story for you to make sure they actually heard the entire thing. If they are unable to satisfactorily describe the flow of the story, read it again.

OPTION B
*Needed: unleavened bread (such as matzo crackers or pita bread), napkins, Bibles*
Prior to reading the story, give each youth a piece of unleavened bread, but instruct them not to eat it yet. Offer them a napkin to put the bread on and hold it in their laps until the appropriate time. Inform them that, toward the end of the story, there is a scene in which bread is broken. At the time the Scripture says that the bread is broken, the youth should take their bread, break it in half, and share half of it with the person next to them. (This means, of course, that each person will be passing a piece to

the person on one side and accepting a piece from the person on the other side.) They may eat the bread after the story is read. Consider using matzo crackers (the large sheets) rather than pita bread, because it will make a wonderful noise when it is broken. Breadsticks or dinner rolls are options if the other items are difficult for you to find.

## Reacting to the Story (10–15 minutes)
OPTION A
*Needed: newsprint and marker or chalkboard and chalk, Bibles, writing paper, writing utensils*
Break the class into three smaller groups (a group can be one person). Assign each group one of the following sections of the Scripture: verses 13-27, verses 28-32, verses 33-35. Make sure everyone has their Bibles, and give each group paper and writing utensils.

Each group is to review their section of the story, verse by verse, and jot notes in the following categories:
■ What questions do you have about this section?
■ What would you like to find out more about?
■ What do you particularly like, find interesting, or connect with?

After the groups have finished, invite them to come back to the larger group and share their results. You will want to do this in order of the sections and take notes on newsprint or chalkboard. Encourage the other youth to review the section quickly while the group is making their presentation.

OPTION B
*Needed: Bibles, construction paper, writing utensils, crayons, newsprint*

*and marker or chalkboard and chalk with sections written out (optional)*

Invite the youth to consider five different moments of the Emmaus road experience:

1. when the disciples are first walking on the road—verses 13-14
2. when the "stranger" approaches them—verses 17-18
3. when the "stranger" corrects them—verses 25-27
4. when their eyes are opened and they recognize Jesus—verses 30-32
5. when they are telling the other disciples what happened—verses 33-35

Write these sections out on newsprint or chalkboard ahead of time.

Explain to the class that they are to consider what the disciples might have been feeling during each of these sections. For each section, youth should each choose a color of construction paper that they think symbolizes that feeling, then draw the facial expression that the disciples may have had during that section. After the drawings are complete, read the Scripture story again and have the youth hold up their drawings for each section while that section is being read. Are there similarities or differences among the drawings? Take a moment to talk about why the youth chose the color they chose and the facial expressions they drew for each section.

### Connecting to the Story (10–15 minutes)

OPTION A
*Needed: construction paper, scissors, crayons or markers, devotional story (optional)*

Invite the youth to discuss the disciples' lack of recognition of Jesus on the road to Emmaus. Why didn't the disciples recognize him? Partway through the discussion, bring into the conversation some of the information from "A Story behind the Story" on the disciples' lack of recognition to find out what the youth think about it. Do they agree or disagree? Then ask the youth:

■ Could we see Christ present in our world? Why or why not?
■ If we could, how would we recognize him? How could we tell that he was present?

Modern-day stories about someone's entertaining Christ without knowing are prevalent. If you know one of these, consider telling it to the youth. Then ask them:

■ Do you believe that kind of thing actually happens? Why or why not?
■ What would it take to help us see Jesus in the world around us?

Give youth construction paper and other supplies, and invite them to create a pair of "Jesus glasses" to help them see Jesus in the world. They are to make a pair of glasses large enough to wear. (Most youth love doing this kind of thing!) They may decorate them in ways that symbolize recognizing Jesus in the world around us.

OPTION B
An old hymn exclaims, "I love to tell the story of Jesus and his love!" But sometimes telling that story is the most uncomfortable thing for a Christian. Despite that, the disciples on the road to Emmaus share the story with someone they think is a total stranger. Now, perhaps at that point it has more of the feel of sharing the local news. They've just

witnessed significant events and are passing these events on to someone who apparently wasn't there. And yet they also share their hope in God's redemption. Then, later, they run to tell the other disciples of their witness to the resurrection.

As Christians, we are also called to share the story. Invite the youth to spend some time discussing why it is difficult for us to share the story of Jesus with folks who haven't heard it (or don't seem to care about it).

- Why should we share the story?
- Under what circumstances should we share the story?
- How could we be more comfortable sharing the story?

## Exploring the Story (10-15 minutes)
OPTION A
*Needed: "Eating with Jesus" handouts, snacks, writing utensils, Bibles*
Obviously, there is something important about food in the Gospels. In the story for this session the disciples recognize Jesus in the act of sharing a meal. The meal takes on Eucharistic tones (that is, it gives us the feel of Communion) as it is cast in the same language used to describe the Last Supper the night before Jesus was crucified.

Give each youth a copy of the "Eating with Jesus" handouts and writing utensils. Make sure they have their Bibles, and offer them snacks to eat while they are working on the handouts. They may choose to work on their handouts in pairs, triads, or other small groupings.

After they've completed the handouts, have them come back into the larger group and share their findings. Ask them if having this information makes them look at eating any differently. Is it only special meals (such as Communion) in which Jesus is present?

OPTION B
*Needed: church tradition for the Eucharist (Communion, or Lord's Supper), Bibles, pastor (optional)*
Ahead of time, gather resources on the way your church celebrates the Lord's Supper. If you can find the wording given for the breaking of the bread and the drinking of the cup, make that available to the youth. Prayer books or worship resources sometimes have these things in them as well. In addition, find resources about your denomination's understanding of Communion, if you can, and offer these to the youth. Consider inviting your pastor into the class to talk about how he or she leads the Eucharist:
- What are the parts of the shared meal (for example, the "invitation to the table," the "prayer of consecration," etc.)?
- Why are these parts included?
- Why are they worded the way they are?
- Is the wording exactly the same every time, or does it change?
- How do we believe Jesus is revealed through the breaking of the bread, as in the Emmaus story?

As part of the discussion, invite the youth to look at what is believed to be the oldest form of the Eucharist in the Bible: 1 Corinthians 11:23-26. What does it mean to proclaim Jesus through the sharing of this meal?

This Scripture is a wonderful opportunity to discuss your

denomination's tradition of Communion with the youth. Allow them to ask any questions they may have.

**Living the Story
(5–10 minutes)**
OPTION A
*Needed: "An Invitation" handouts, Bibles, writing utensils, CD player and CD (optional)*
Point out to the youth the part of the story in which Jesus "walked ahead" (verse 28). Explain that many scholars believe this points out how Jesus waits for an invitation to enter into one's life rather than forcing his presence upon someone unready to accept it. Take a few moments to discuss this concept with the youth. Do they see it in the Scripture? Do they agree?

Give each one of them a copy of "An Invitation" handout, their Bibles, and writing utensils. Consider playing some background music as they do their work. This is quiet, private work, so ensure that the youth do not distract each other or violate anyone's privacy. Encourage them to stay silent throughout their individual work.

When everyone has had a chance to complete as much as they choose of the handout, instruct them to put the handouts someplace where they'll remember to take them home. Invite them to come into a circle, standing and holding hands. Share in a closing prayer together, thanking God for the opportunity to have God's Son revealed to us.

OPTION B
*Needed: worship planning resources, Bibles, pastor (optional)*

Have your youth review everything they've discussed about table fellowship and the Lord's Supper during this session. Invite them to share any new insights they have.

Offer them the worship planning resources, and invite the class to plan a Communion celebration of some sort. If your tradition requires a member of the clergy to officiate at the Eucharist, invite that person to be a part of the planning, and help the youth plan the remainder of the service. What kinds of elements to the service would they want to include, reflecting some of their learnings from the session? What songs might they sing? What Scriptures might be read?

Be sure to pray your way through the planning, and make sure to set a date for the service itself. Close your session with prayer, expressing thanks for the revelation of God that we have received through Jesus Christ.

**Things to Ponder**
This session offers an opportunity for youth to do some serious thinking about inviting Jesus into their lives. But help youth feel accepted by you regardless of where they are on their faith journeys. Not all youth are ready to make a full-time commitment to Christ. Follow up as appropriate with youth who appear open to Jesus.

**Looking Ahead**
For the next session, you may need a collection of religious magazines. Consider asking other church members to help you create a large assortment.

# Eating with Jesus

*There's lots of food stuff going on in the Bible. Is our understanding of food and eating together different because we're Christians? Read the following Scriptures and fill in the chart. Then answer the questions at the bottom.*

**Matthew 9:9-13**          **Mark 6:30-44**          **Luke 12:35-37**

**John 6:32-35**          **1 Corinthians 11:23-26**          **Revelation 3:20**

*For each Scripture, give the following information:*

| | Who is eating? | Who is serving? | What food? | What does it mean? |
|---|---|---|---|---|
| **1.** | | | | |
| **2.** | | | | |
| **3.** | | | | |
| **4.** | | | | |
| **5.** | | | | |
| **6.** | | | | |

**1.** With whom do you think Jesus feels we should eat? (That is, with whom should we sit down at a table?)

**2.** Why is eating with someone so important to Jesus?

**3.** Have you ever shared a table with a stranger? With someone with whom you might not normally choose to share a table? Was it easy or difficult? Why?

**4.** When is Jesus present at a meal?

# An Invitation

**Dear Jesus,**

**I would like to invite you to . . .**

**Love,**

# 14. By Faith

*Bible Story: Hebrews 11:1–12:2*

Dotty Luera

## A Story behind the Story

Hebrews 11:1–12:2 begins with a definition of faith and goes on to describe many Old Testament saints who lived by faith. Noah, Abraham, Moses, Isaac, and Jacob are just a few of the characters whose actions of faith are described in the passage. In Hebrews 11:32, however, we find the names of several more people of faith listed without descriptions of what they did. Those descriptions can be found in the Old Testament. The story of Gideon, a hero of the Manasseh tribe who drove out the invading Midianites, destroyed an altar of Baal, and created an *ephod* (a kind of image that later became an idol), is told in Judges 6–8. The story of Barak, the leader of Judge Deborah's great army, is told in Judges 4–5. The story of Samson, who had been given tremendous strength by God but gave in to Delilah, losing his strength, is told in Judges 13–16. The story of Jephthah, a mighty warrior who was called from exile to lead his people against the Ammonite oppression and who later hastily made a promise to God and had to sacrifice his own daughter, is found in Judges 11–12. The story of Samuel, a prophet, judge, and priest who anointed the first king of Israel, is told in 1 Samuel 8–11. The story of David, the second king of Israel, slaying the giant Goliath is told in 1 Samuel 17. The story of David capturing Jerusalem and moving the ark of the covenant to its new location is told in 2 Samuel 5–6. The story of David becoming involved with another man's wife, Bathsheba, is told in 2 Samuel 11.

In the last verses of Hebrews 11 we read of the courageous actions of unnamed people of faith. Some of these descriptions may seem familiar and remind us of other Bible heroes who lived their faith. Daniel may come to mind as we read verse 33 ("shut the mouths of lions"). We may be reminded of Paul and Silas as we read verse 36 ("Others suffered mocking and flogging, and even chains and imprisonment"). We may be reminded of Stephen as we read verse 37 ("They were stoned to death"). This great cloud of witnesses fills us with awe and great inspiration as we strive to run with perseverance the race that is set before us (Hebrews 12:1).

## Enter the Story

"Faith is the assurance of things hoped for, the conviction of things not seen" (Hebrews 11:1). This is the beginning verse of our Bible story for the week. The passage goes on to describe people of faith. Are we people of faith?

Find a quiet place and a time to be alone and reflect upon the story. Are the characters mentioned familiar to you? Will the characters be familiar to the youth in your group? Do you identify with one of the people mentioned? Will the youth in your group be

## POSSIBLE YOUTH CONTACT POINTS

- What is faith?
- Do I have faith?
- How do my actions demonstrate my faith?
- What pleases God?
- Do I please God?

## YOU MAY NEED

- adhesive name tags or small pieces of paper and straight pins
- list of questions and answers about the people of faith mentioned in Hebrews 11
- writing utensils
- paper
- Bibles
- strips of paper with the name of each of the characters listed in Hebrews 11
- "People of Faith" handouts
- mustard seeds
- "Demonstrations of Faith" handouts
- objects that symbolize those things where people often put their faith–other than God (see Option B, "Connecting to the Story")
- Bible study helps
- collection of religious magazines
- ribbon

able to identify with any of the characters?

Take time to consider your own faith. Do you trust in the rich promises of God? Think about the youth in your group. Where might they be in their faith journeys?

Pray and think deeply about this story. Ask God to be with you as you prepare and with the youth as they interpret the story.

## Setting the Stage (5–10 minutes)

OPTION A

*Needed: adhesive name tags or small pieces of paper, straight pins*

Before the session begins, write the name of one of the people listed in today's Scripture on each name tag or small piece of paper. As youth enter the room, greet each one and ask about their week. Place one of the names on their back without allowing them to see it. Explain to each youth that today you will be talking about people of faith. You have placed the name of such a person on their back. They will be looking at the names on the backs of the other youth. Without telling the name, they will help each other discover their identity by giving clues. Some clues might include the following:

- How are Rachel and Leah getting along?
- Looks like rain!
- Is the Red Sea really red?
- How do you make a slingshot?
- Tell Sarah that I asked about her.

Allow time for youth to walk around and converse with each other, giving helpful clues. As youth discover the name of their

person of faith, they may remove the name tag. Everyone may continue to give clues until all tags are removed.

OPTION B

*Needed: a list of questions and answers about the people of faith listed in today's Scripture, egg timer*

Welcome each youth as they enter the room. Allow time and opportunity for youth to visit with each other. Explain to the youth that today you will be playing a version of the popular television game *The Weakest Link*. You will be asking them questions about people of faith from the Bible. They will not be voting each other out of the game but simply seeing how many questions they can answer correctly in a two-minute period.

Invite the youth to stand in a semicircle while you stand in the center. Set the timer for two minutes. Call each youth by name and ask one of the questions you have prepared. If they answer correctly, tell them they are correct. If they are incorrect, respond with the correct answer and move on to the next youth. You may wish to prepare some simple questions as well as some more difficult ones. Questions might include:

- Who received the coat of many colors?
- What sea parted for the Israelites?
- Who was Jacob's true love?

Encourage the youth to have fun. They can shout out their answers and cheer each other on.

## Telling the Story
## (5–10 minutes)

OPTION A

*Needed: writing utensils, paper*

Suggest that the youth gather around a table and be seated for this activity in order for them to be able to write more easily. Give each youth a writing utensil and a piece of paper. Tell the youth that you will be reading Hebrews 11:1–12:2 to them. Encourage them to listen carefully as you read the passage. Explain that today's Bible story contains the names of many people of faith. Invite the youth to write down the names as they hear them and also jot down the ways that each person may have demonstrated his or her faith.

Begin reading the story aloud, giving special attention to the names the youth will hear. As you conclude the story, allow plenty of time for the youth to finish their writing.

OPTION B

*Needed: Bibles for each youth, strips of paper with the name of each of the characters mentioned in today's Bible story written on them*

Give a Bible to each youth so that they may participate in this activity. Tell the youth that the Bible story today is from Hebrews 11:1–12:2. Invite them to locate this passage in their Bible. Explain that you will be leading them in a reader's theater and that this Scripture is filled with people who lived by faith. Assign one of the characters in today's story to each youth who would like to read by giving him or her one of the strips of paper. Invite the youth

to scan through the passage, locating their assigned character. Allow a few moments for youth to do this.

Explain that you will now stand and begin reading. Invite the youth to follow along in their Bibles. When you come to a particular character and the youth hear the words *by faith,* the youth who has been assigned that character will stand and read aloud. Then, when that volunteer has finished reading the scripture section related to his or her person of faith, the volunteer may sit down. As you have followed the reading, you will be ready to introduce the next character with the words "by faith." You may continue in this pattern and conclude the story by reading the last verses yourself.

Some youth may be eager to read aloud to the group, while others may be more reluctant. Be sensitive to their needs.

## Reacting to the Story
## (15–20 minutes)

OPTION A

*(If you chose Option A under "Telling the Story" above, you may wish to choose the following exercise for this segment.)*

*Needed: Bibles for each youth, writing utensils, " People of Faith" handouts*

Begin by inviting youth to share the lists they made as you read the Bible story in Option A above. Some youth may have different names or longer lists than others. Allow each volunteer the opportunity to speak.

Give each youth a Bible, a writing utensil, and a copy of the handout "People of Faith." Invite the youth to look at the handout with you. Notice that there are two sections. The first section asks the question *Which characters in this passage have you heard of before?* Encourage youth to write the names of those characters. If they are not familiar with any of the names, they may leave it blank. The second section of the handout asks, "With whom do you most identify?" Invite youth to look over the passage and choose a character with whom they identify. Who caught their attention? How might they relate to this person of faith?

Allow time for your youth to reflect and write their answers. Invite them to share their responses with the group.

OPTION B

*Needed: Bibles for each youth, pencils, paper, mustard seeds*

Ask the youth to think about the people of faith whom you read about today. Invite them to select a character who caught their attention. Allow a few moments for the youth to make their decisions and then encourage them to share their selections with the group. Ask youth to team up with others who have chosen the same character. If the groupings are too large, you might wish to divide them into teams of two or three. There may be more than one group with the same name. Tell your youth that they are now invited to participate in the prestigious new Mustard Seed Awards!

Invite the youth to brainstorm with their partners and write a brief introduction of their person of faith. Encourage them to use their imagination and be creative. They may wish to add information or simply use what is in the passage. Explain that one (or two, if there is a total of three) of the partners will do the presentation and the other partner will accept the prestigious Mustard Seed.

Allow time for youth to write their presentations and decide who will present and who will receive. After they have finished their preparations, you might wish to begin the ceremony by reading from Matthew 17:20, where faith is compared to a mustard seed.

Encourage the youth to have fun. Cheer for and applaud each participant!

## Connecting to the Story (15–20 minutes)

OPTION A

*Needed: Bibles for each youth, writing utensils, "Demonstrations of Faith" handouts*

Give each youth a Bible, a pencil, and a copy of the handout "Demonstrations of Faith." Ask them all to look at the handout with you. They will notice that several of the characters from today's Bible story are listed. Invite the youth to consider how each of these characters demonstrated faith. Then encourage the youth to use their Bibles as references and to answer the following questions.

■ How did this person of faith please God?

■ What actions did this person of faith take?

■ What was God's response to this person?

Allow adequate time for youth to complete this portion of the handout.

When they have finished writing, invite your youth to reflect upon the ways that they, themselves, demonstrate faith. They may wish to consider the same questions.

- How do I please God?
- What actions do I take in my own faith journey?
- What is God's response to me?

Encourage youth to think deeply about their responses and to record them on the handout. When they have finished, invite youth to share their thoughts with the group.

OPTION B
*Needed: objects that symbolize those things that people often put their faith in—other than God*
Before youth arrive, select items that symbolize things that people put their faith in—other than God. Some examples might be a wallet (money), a report card (good grades or education), friendship bracelet (friends), wine glass (alcohol), wedding ring (spouse), car keys (their set of wheels), office memo or letterhead (career), and a photo album (family). Lay out these items so that they are easily seen.

Invite your youth to reflect upon today's Bible story and how the characters in it demonstrated their faith in God. You may wish to ask youth for examples by asking questions about specific characters.

- How did Moses demonstrate his faith in God?
- How did Noah demonstrate his faith?
- How did Abraham demonstrate his faith?

Now ask the youth to consider how people often put their faith in things other than God. Invite them to look at the objects you have displayed and to each select a different item. Allow time for them to make their selections. Then encourage your youth to share what they think each item might represent. Finally, invite the youth to think about where they put their faith.

## Exploring the Story
## (15–20 minutes)
OPTION A
*Needed: Bible for each youth, Bible study aids, collection of religious magazines (such as* Guideposts, Group Magazine, Upper Room), *denominational magazines, pencils, and paper*
Suggest that your youth gather around a table and be seated for this activity in order for them to be able to write more easily. Give each youth a Bible, a pencil, and paper. Place the Bible study aids within easy reach of all the youth. Invite each to work with a partner for this activity. Explain that you will be learning more about each of the persons of faith from today's Bible story.

Assign one of the characters to each team. Encourage the youth to use their Bibles and the study aids to find information about their assigned character and to jot down their thoughts. How did this person act upon her or his faith?

Then invite youth to look through the magazines and see if they might discover the story of a person who demonstrated faith in a similar way. You may wish to give them an illustration. For example, Noah lived through a catastrophic time, but others have also survived disasters by placing their faith in God. Also, just as Moses led the Israelites out of slavery, so Abraham Lincoln issued the Emancipation Proclamation and freed the slaves in America. Encourage your youth to enjoy their faith explorations as they make new discoveries.

When the youth have finished writing, allow volunteers to share their stories with the group.

## OPTION B
*Needed: Bibles for each youth, Bible study helps, pencils, and paper*

Give a Bible, pencil, and paper to each youth. Place the Bible study resources within easy reach of all youth. Have each work with a partner or in teams (according to the size of your group) for this activity. Invite the youth to explore the persons of faith named but not described in Hebrews 11:32. Assign one of the characters—Gideon, Barak, Samson, Jephthah, Samuel, or David—to each of the teams. Encourage the youth to discover the faith story of their assigned character. How did this person's actions reflect his or her faith?
How did this person please God?
How did God respond to this person of faith?

Allow time for the youth to explore and make their discoveries. When they have finished, invite volunteers to share what they have learned with the group.

## Living the Story
## (5–10 minutes)
OPTION A
*Needed: a piece of ribbon for each youth*

Read the statement of encouragement from Hebrews 12:1—"let us run with perseverance the race that is set before us"—to the group. Challenge the youth to live out their faith. You may wish to give examples, such as becoming a volunteer for Habitat for Humanity. Your neighborhood may have a local food pantry in need of help with stocking or distributing food. Perhaps youth could join SADD (Students Against Drunk Driving) at their school or become a peer counselor. They might be interested in visiting a nursing home or a local children's hospital or day care center. Encourage youth to offer their own ideas of living out their faith. You may decide to act as a group and plan a day of service or you may challenge youth to work individually.

When you have decided on a course of action, invite your youth to gather in a closing circle with you. Explain that you would like to commission them to go out and live their faith in the way they have chosen. Approach each youth and tie the ribbon onto their shoelace or around their ankle, signifying the race that is set before them, and then say to them, "Run with perseverance, looking to Jesus." When you have commissioned each youth, you may close with a prayer, asking God to lead and guide all of you in your faith journeys.

OPTION B

To close this session, encourage the youth in their faith journeys. You may wish to remind them that even the persons of faith in our Bible story today struggled as they met with obstacles. Moses never entered the Promised Land. Samson gave in to Delilah. David gave in to lust. Jephthah made a hasty promise to God and ended up sacrificing his own daughter. Gideon made a religious symbol that eventually became an idol. Invite the youth to think about the struggles in their own faith journey. Allow time and opportunity for volunteers to share their experiences with the group.

Invite the youth to join you in a closing circle of prayer. Ask God for strength and courage as you face challenges in your faith journeys.

## Things to Ponder

This week's Bible story is lengthy and contains much information. It is filled with stories of faith from the Old Testament. Many of the names of these people of faith may be familiar to some youth in your group. Other youth, however, may not know any of these Old Testament faith stories. Be sensitive to each level of learning. As youth hear of the struggles of some of these characters, they may choose to share their own stories with the group. Be open and caring as youth reflect upon their faith journeys.

## Looking Ahead

The next session has several possibilities for intergenerational learning. Be sure to read the session enough in advance to provide plenty of time for inviting adults into the session.

# People of Faith

**Hebrews 11**

Which characters in this passage have you heard of before?

With whom do you most identify? Why?

# Demonstrations of Faith

| | How did this person of faith please God? | What actions did this person of faith take? | What was God's response to this person? |
|---|---|---|---|
| **Abel** | | | |
| **Noah** | | | |
| **Abraham** | | | |
| **Moses** | | | |

# 15. God's Faithfulness

*Bible Story: Psalm 105*

**Lisa and Chris Holliday**

### A Story behind the Story

This historical psalm summarizes the story of the Israelites from God's initial covenant with Abraham to God's giving of the Promised Land. It was probably written during or after the period of Babylonian exile. God's people are in need of hope. If still in exile, they are wondering whether they will possess the Promised Land again. If during the time of resettlement back in Judah, they are wondering how they will rebuild the temple and everything else that has been destroyed. In either case, they are wondering whether they will be able to preserve their identity as God's chosen people.

During this crucial time, the people need to remember God's faithfulness and the ways in which God has delivered them in the past. They need to remember the kept covenants. They need to remember the miracles of God and feel awe and wonder. They need to recapture the surprise and gratefulness their ancestors experienced over the plagues of Egypt and the provisions God gave in the wilderness. They need to recall God's faithfulness to Jacob and his family, particularly concerning Joseph. They need to remember the way God cared for Abraham and the covenants God made with him, especially the one giving the Promised Land to Abraham's descendants (verse 11). Finally, they need to remember the victorious taking of Canaan and the time of wealth and prosperity.

Why do the people need to remember? The psalmist seems to have several reasons in mind. Such remembrance educates the people about their past, helps them keep their identity as the people of God, and promotes their obedience to God. It encourages the people to respond to God with all that they have and all that they are, and it rekindles trust in God and God's faithfulness.

The psalmist also tries to impress upon the people the importance of expressing gratitude and praise to God for all God has done. In fact, Psalm 105 falls into the category of psalms referred to as "psalms of praise," including both an invitation to praise and the reasons laid out for praising.

Finally, the psalmist hopes to help the people cope with the present and anticipate the future. What new possibilities await God's people? Where would they go from here?

### Enter the Story

Knowing the story of the Israelites can help us in many of the same ways that it was intended to help the Judeans returning from exile. We, too, need to remember God's faithfulness to God's people from Abraham to the present. We, too, need to remember the miracles and wonders of God both past and present. We need to praise God and to offer our whole selves to God's service. Like the Israelites, we need to trust in God concerning our present and our future.

As one of God's people, spend some time this week considering God's faithfulness to you, your family, and your church community. How has God kept covenant with you? How has God delivered you from oppression and pain? How do you plan to be obedient to God in the present and future? When do you best experience the awe and wonder of God? Take time to praise God this week for all that God has done for you.

NOTE: All of the Option A's in this lesson provide the opportunity for intergenerational interaction. Having adult church members participate, especially ones who have been in the church for some time, could be interesting and enlightening for the youth. This interaction will also live out the biblical themes of God's relationship through history with generations of God's people.

## Setting the Stage (5–10 minutes)

OPTION A

*Needed: newsprint and markers, adult volunteers (optional— see note above)*

Before the session, write and display the following question on newsprint and ask everyone entering to consider it: "What was your most memorable _____, and why?" Underneath the question, list subjects like "vacation," "birthday," "experience in school," "experience related to sports," "experience related to music," "experience at work." After the group has gath-

ered, ask each person to mentally fill in the blank and to share his or her response.

Once everyone has finished sharing, say something like: *Remembering key past experiences is very important for individuals and communities. These experiences become our history, and they say a lot about who we are and what we believe. Today we're going to look at several histories, starting with a summary of the history of the Israelites.*

OPTION B

*Needed: paper sign for each youth's back, tape*

Before the session, prepare a paper sign for each youth's back. Half of the signs should name important people in history (one person per sign). Each of the remaining signs should name an important historical event in which one of the people was involved. For example, one youth could have "Abraham Lincoln" on his back and another could have "The Civil War." Other examples are "Watergate" and "Richard Nixon"; "Eve" and "The Creation Story."

Explain to the youth: *I am going to place a sign on each of your backs. Some of the signs will name important people in history and some will name important events. Each person has a match. Thus, if your sign has a person on it, there is an event listed on another person's back with which that person was involved, and vice versa. To find out who or what event you are, you can ask others yes-or-no questions only. Once you know who or what event you are, you can find your match*

## POSSIBLE YOUTH CONTACT POINTS

- **Am I one of God's people?**
- **How has God been faithful to me and my family?**
- **How does our church's history show God's faithfulness?**
- **Why isn't trusting in God easier for me?**
- **Where is God when I go through rough times?**
- **How do I praise God?**

## YOU MAY NEED

- Bibles
- newsprint and markers
- Bible study resources
- several different translations of the Bible, including at least one contemporary paraphrase, such as *The Message* (Eugene Peterson, NavPress, 2000)
- writing utensils
- blank paper
- one adult church member per youth (each youth could ask a person of his or her choice)
- church historian (optional)
- paper sign for each youth's back
- tape
- hymnals or chorus books
- large roll of bulletin board paper
- several tables and chairs
- "How God Has Been Faithful" handouts
- "My Family History" handouts
- closing song

*and tell him or her that you're the match. The other person still has to guess who he or she is, though, through yes-or-no questions.*

After the game is completed, tell the youth that remembering people and events from the past is very important for individuals and communities. These experiences become our history, and they say a lot about who we are and who we've become. Explain that in this session you are going to look at a summary of the history of the Israelites.

## Telling the Story (5–10 minutes)
OPTION A
*Needed: Bibles, adult volunteers (optional)*
Divide the youth into smaller groups of three to four. Ask each small group to prepare a skit or dramatic reading for one or more of the following sections:

- verses 1-6
- verses 7-11
- verses 12-15
- verses 16-22
- verses 23-25
- verses 26-36
- verses 37-41
- verses 42-45

Make sure all the sections are covered. Not all the groups have to be the same size. Some passages could be performed well by one or two people, while others could benefit from more people. If needed, some groups could perform more than one section.

As part of their preparation, have the groups see if they can come up with a title for their section that would capture its main theme.

After the groups' preparation time, ask them to share their presentations with the large group in the order of the Scripture. Then read Psalm 105 aloud in its entirety.

OPTION B
*Needed: Bibles, hymnals or chorus books, several translations of the Bible, paper, writing utensils*
Tell the youth that the Book of Psalms is a collection of poems, prayers, and songs that have been sung for a very long time. Ask if anyone knows of a psalm or part of a psalm that they've sung or heard sung. After youth's responses, hand out hymnals or chorus books and ask your class to look in the index of scriptural quotations (usually found in the back of such books) and to name some of the psalms that are used as words for hymns or choruses. As a group, examine a few of the hymns or choruses and their corresponding psalms in the Bible to see how close the words are and how the psalm has been arranged musically. Sing a few of the songs to experience the psalm-to-music connection.

Read Psalm 105 aloud to the group. Split the youth into small groups and ask each group to write a song or rap of Psalm 105. Allow them to change the words somewhat if they need to do so. It may also be helpful to have several translations of the Bible available, including a contemporary paraphrase such as *The Message,* to aid the youth in this project. Encourage the youth to be creative and to involve all the members of their group in some way. Once they've had time to prepare, gather the youth back into the large group and have each group perform their song or rap.

## Reacting to the Story (15–20 minutes)
OPTION A
*Needed: large roll of bulletin board paper, several tables and chairs, markers, tape, adult volunteers (optional)*
Take a large roll of bulletin board paper and roll it out on several tables. Ask each small group from "Telling the Story," Option A, to stay together. Invite the small group with verses 1-6 to come and sit down in front of the leftmost portion of the paper. Then ask the small group with verses 7-11 to sit beside the first group. Continue this process until the last group (verses 42-45) is seated at the far right end of the table. If some groups are doing more than one section, ask them to do each section in the appropriate place on the paper.

Have markers available for all the groups. Ask each group to help create a giant mural of Psalm 105 by drawing pictures or symbols of their verses on their portion of the mural. Ask them to consider the historical significance of the events listed and to highlight the significant words and phrases from their passages by writing them on their drawings or by symbolizing them in some way.

Once the process is completed, ask each group to share their part(s) of the mural and to share the words, phrases, and events from their verses that seemed most

important to them. Finally, hang the mural on the wall so that all can see it during the rest of the session.

OPTION B
*Needed: newsprint and markers*
Most of the youth have probably heard of television cable channel VH1's *Behind the Music* series. Each episode tells the story of a group of musicians and their journey through the ups and downs of life. Tell the group that they are going to go "behind the psalm" later to examine the people and situations both within and behind the psalm.

In preparation for that project, ask the youth to come up with as many questions as they can about the passage. Are there words that they do not understand? Are there stories that don't make sense to them? Do they understand who all the characters in the story are? Do they know when this psalm was written, for whom it was written, and why? Tell them that all questions are valid and encourage the youth to be affirming of each other as they share their questions. Write all their responses on newsprint and save the newsprint for "Exploring the Story," Option B.

## Connecting to the Story (15–20 minutes)
OPTION A
*Needed: one adult church member per youth, "How God Has Been Faithful" handouts, writing utensils, newsprint and marker*
Ask each youth to find an adult partner. (If each youth brought an adult, then the adult whom the

youth brought would be his or her partner.) Give everyone a "How God Has Been Faithful" handout and a pencil. Ask the youth partner to interview the adult partner first and to record the adult's name and responses on the handout. Then ask the adult to interview the youth and do the same. Tell them that when they come back together as the large group, the youth will report on the adult's comments and the adult will report on the youth's comments. Hopefully this section will encourage relationships between the youth and the adults and help them see that we all rely on God's grace and provision in our lives. As each partner talks about the church, the group should also start to see some similarities between the biblical story in Psalm 105 and the story of their own church.

After the pairs have had time to interview each other, bring the group together and ask each person to share his or her partner's thoughts. List all the responses to the second question on a piece of newsprint entitled "God's Faithfulness to Our Church." This newsprint will be used in Option A of both "Exploring the Story" and "Living the Story."

OPTION B
*Needed: "My Family History" handouts, writing utensils, paper*
Give everyone a "My Family History" handout and a writing utensil. Point out the historical nature of Psalm 105, and explain that the history is of a "family" of people. Ask the youth to write as much as they know about the history of their families. Have them highlight times

when they believe God was faithful to their families and to them. Invite the youth to start as far back in time as they can.

Once they are finished, ask them to find a partner and to share with that person some of what they've written. After the partners have shared, ask each pair to come up with a way to praise God for all God has done in the lives of their families. They could draw a picture, write a poem, create a cheer, perform a pantomime, or do anything else they can think of. Gather the large group and ask each pair to share their ways of praise.

## Exploring the Story (15–20 minutes)
OPTION A
*Needed: Bibles, newsprint and markers, "God's Faithfulness to Our Church" newsprint, church historian (optional)*
Say to the group: *Now that we've discussed how God has been faithful to us and to our church, let's go back to the psalm and discuss how God was faithful to the Israelites.* Write on the top of a fresh piece of newsprint the following: "God's Faithfulness to the Israelites." Invite the group to find the stories mentioned in Psalm 105 in their longer forms in the Bible and to examine the stories in more depth (like the story of Joseph). Also, share information from "A Story behind the Story" to help the group consider God's faithfulness to the generation for whom the psalm was originally written. Explore each section of Psalm 105 and write all the responses on newsprint.

Then ask the church historian or the group to add to the newsprint from "Connecting to the Story," Option A, any other major ways that God has been faithful to your church. Finally, discuss the similarities and the differences between the two newsprint lists.

OPTION B
*Needed: "Behind the Psalm" newsprint, markers*
Tell the youth that it's time to go behind the psalm. Summarize the information from "A Story behind the Story." Then display the newsprint of questions from "Reacting to the Story," Option B, so that all the youth can see. Divide the youth into small groups or pairs and evenly divide the questions between the groups. Make Bible study resources available and ask them to explore their assigned questions. Walk around and assist the youth as needed. Encourage the group to find the stories mentioned in Psalm 105 in their longer forms in the Bible and to examine the stories in more depth (like the story of Joseph) to help them with applicable questions. Also invite the youth to research other questions that come up as they explore. Finally, ask each group to come up with a fun, VH1 sort of way to report their information.

Once all the groups have completed their research, have each pair or small group share their findings with the large group. Then ask:
■ From all you know about the Israelites, were they faithful to God? How or how not?
■ Was God faithful to the Israelites? How or how not?

## Living the Story
## (5–10 minutes)
OPTION A
*Needed: church historian (optional), "God's Faithfulness to Our Church" newsprint, paper, writing utensils, closing song*
Give the church historian a few minutes to share any special pictures or memorabilia that he or she might have concerning the church. Then divide into small groups. Display the "God's Faithfulness to Our Church" newsprint so all can see. Ask each group to come up with a psalm about your church. They can tell the history of the church, highlight those times when God's faithfulness has shown brilliantly through, and praise God for all God has done for the church. Ask each group to title their psalm and to be prepared to sing, rap, or dramatically read it. After the groups are finished, bring them back together and have each group share their psalm.

Then form a circle and hold hands. Thank everyone for participating and affirm them for their sharing. Sing a hymn such as "Great Is Thy Faithfulness." Then conclude with a prayer praising and thanking God for God's faithfulness.

OPTION B
*Needed: closing song*
Tell the youth: *Life experiences—of individuals or of groups—can help us better respond to the present and future. In other words, our past can inform our present and future. We've spent some time today discussing the story of the Israelite people who became the*

*Judeans and who were exiled to Babylon. Some of them eventually came back to Jerusalem to renew their covenants with God and to try to become a more faithful people. Psalms like Psalm 105 offered hope to these exiles returning home. God had been faithful all along, even when the Israelites had not been. Thus they had hope for a better future.*

Ask the group the following questions and discuss the responses among the group:

■ Do your past encounters with God give you hope for your future? Why or why not?

■ As you consider your family histories and as you consider God's faithfulness to the Israelites, for what are you grateful?

■ How about our church? Has God been faithful to us? How or how not?

■ On a scale of 1 to 10 (1 being the lowest and 10 being the highest), how much do you trust God? Explain why.

Sing a song such as "Great Is Thy Faithfulness." Then close with a circle prayer in which each person praises God for one thing for which he or she is grateful.

**Things to Ponder**

Did the youth understand that they are connected to the people in the biblical story? Continue to help them understand that they, too, are part of the family of God. Did they recognize God's faithfulness in their lives? Were any youth upset as they talked about their family histories? Pray for each youth this week, and follow up as appropriate.

Also, some of the youth may have begun to bond with their adult partners today. If you do not have a mentoring program, consider starting one. Mentoring can be a meaningful and enriching experience for all involved.

**Looking Ahead**

For the next session, you will need to find a recording of the song "How Majestic Is Your Name!" It has been done by several artists. Searching for the title on the Internet or checking at your local Christian bookstore should enable you to find a recording.

# How God Has Been Faithful

**Partner's name:** _____

How has God been faithful to you in your life?

How has God been faithful to this church over the years?

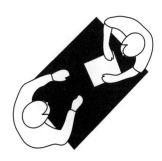

# My Family History

# 16. How Majestic Is Your Name!

*Bible Story: Psalm 8*

Dotty Luera

## A Story behind the Story

The Book of Psalms is a treasury of religious poems. It is often described as the hymnbook of Israel. Most of the psalms were probably written to be used in worship, and approximately half of the psalms are attributed to David. You will notice that the words "A Psalm of David" appear many times. Our Scripture reading for this week, Psalm 8, is introduced in this way. (The word *Selah* is often seen in the psalms as well. It appears over seventy times! *Selah* is a musical direction and suggests an interlude or pause.)

The Book of Psalms is divided into five sections or books. Book I consists of Psalms 1–41, Book II consists of Psalms 42–72, Book III consists of Psalms 73–89, Book IV consists of Psalms 90–106, and Book V consists of Psalms 107–150. The writing and compilation of Psalms was a long process, beginning around 1000 BCE and perhaps extending through 400 BCE. Many authors are implied as new collections were added. Therefore, the words "A Psalm of David" should be understood as an honorific statement rather than a statement of actual authorship.

The psalms express an incredible variety of religious experiences—from painful struggles with illness and difficulties to heartfelt songs of thanksgiving. The two broad categories of praises and laments include most of the psalms. A lament is a prayer to God asking for help. Some laments are petitions by individuals, as seen in Psalm 61, and they use the first-person singular. Other laments are petitions by a community or a group, as seen in Psalm 60.

The psalm that we are reading this week, Psalm 8, is a song of praise and celebration. It is addressed to the choirmaster in many translations, and the beginning verse is repeated at the end as a refrain. According to this psalm, the glory of God can be seen in the songs of children (verse 2) and also in the night sky (verse 3). It celebrates God's glory and celebrates God's gift to us as well. God has given us dominion over the rest of creation (verses 5-8). How magnificent of God to share with us this authority! As we reflect on this honor that God has bestowed upon us, we are also reminded of the responsibility that God has given to us. The works of God's hands are in ours.

## Enter the Story

Begin your preparation for this session by praying. Thank God for the words that you will read and ask for understanding and guidance. Feel God's presence as you listen for direction and read the story.

Our Scripture for this session is Psalm 8. Are you familiar with any of the psalms? Perhaps you have read or heard Psalm 23 or Psalm 100. Perhaps the youth who will be attending this session are familiar with some of the psalms also.

Read Psalm 8 silently and then read it aloud. Notice that the beginning sentence and the ending sentence are the same, as in a refrain.

## POSSIBLE YOUTH CONTACT POINTS

- **What is my place in God's creation?**
- **What responsibilities do I have in God's creation?**
- **How can I praise God?**
- **Why should I praise God?**

## YOU MAY NEED

- small paper cups
- variety of flower seeds
- potting soil
- water
- writing utensils
- paper
- cassette or CD player
- any recording of the song "How Majestic Is Your Name!"
- colored pencils or crayons
- "My Psalm" handouts
- Bibles
- newsprint and marker
- Bible commentaries
- Bible dictionary
- "God's Creation" handouts
- chalkboard or newsprint
- chalk or markers

Have you ever heard these words put to music or sung?

This particular psalm is a song of praise and celebration. Have you ever tried writing a song or poem? Would the youth who will be attending this session enjoy composing their own psalm? Be open to youth who might enjoy this form of creative expression.

### Setting the Stage (5–10 minutes)

Greet the youth as they come into the room. Allow them the opportunity to greet each other as well. Invite the youth to sit down and to visit with one another. You might ask the youth about their week and whether they would like to share some particular good news or celebration with the group. Begin by sharing a celebration of your own. Lead the youth in an opening prayer of praise, thanking God for any good news they have shared.

### OPTION A

*Needed: small paper cups, a variety of flower seeds, potting soil, water*
As you prepare the youth to hear today's story of Creation, invite the youth to plant a flower. Suggest that the youth gather around a table where all of the supplies are readily available. Give each of the youth a small paper cup. Invite them to fill it halfway with potting soil and then choose the type of flower they would like to grow. After they have made their selections, invite the youth to push the seeds into the soil, adding more soil (if needed) and a small amount of water. The youth may wish to label their cups

with the name of the flower they have planted and also with the date. You may wish to encourage the youth to take their plants home with them or you may wish to keep the plants in your classroom and care for them each week together.

### OPTION B

*Needed: pencils, blank sheets of paper or large index cards*
As you prepare the youth to hear today's Bible story, give each youth a pencil and a sheet of paper or a large index card. Ask the youth to reflect on the following questions:

- What are some of your responsibilities?
- Who are you responsible to?
- What consequences are involved if you don't follow through?

Encourage the youth to spend a few moments thinking about their answers before writing them on the paper that you have provided. Allow time for the youth to record their responses.

When all youth have finished writing, ask for volunteers to share their thoughts. Some youth may be eager to share with the group, while others may not. Give each volunteer the opportunity to speak.

### Telling the Story (5–10 minutes)

OPTION A
*Needed: pencils, paper, cassette or CD player, recording of "How Majestic Is Your Name!"*
Suggest that youth gather around a table and be seated for this activity in order for them to be able to write more easily. Give each youth a pencil and a piece of paper. Explain to

the youth that today you will be reading Psalm 8. Invite youth to listen carefully as you read and to decide whether any of this passage seems familiar to them. Have they ever heard any of the words or phrases before? Does it perhaps remind them of another story? Encourage the youth to jot down their thoughts. Read the Scripture aloud, giving consideration to punctuation and rhythm. When you have completed reading the story, allow a few moments for the youth to finish writing.

Tell the youth that you would like for them to listen to a recording now. Explain that as they are listening they should write down words and phrases that they have just heard in the Bible passage you read to them. Play the song "How Majestic Is Your Name!" When the song has ended, allow time for the youth to complete their notes.

OPTION B
*Needed: colored pencils or crayons, paper*
The youth may wish to gather around a table and be seated for this activity in order for them to be able to participate more easily. Make sure that each youth has access to the colored pencils or crayons and a piece of paper. Explain to the youth that today you will be reading Psalm 8 to them twice. Invite the youth to listen to the passage the first time without doing anything except entertaining the images that it brings to mind. Then encourage the youth to listen as you read the passage a second time and invite them to sketch a

picture of God's creation as they interpret it from the story.

Encourage the youth to relax and enjoy the images as they see them and not to be concerned about the quality of their artwork. Some youth may be reluctant to draw or share their picture. Be sensitive to the needs of the youth as you encourage them to participate. Allow time for the youth to finish their sketches.

**Reacting to the Story
(15–20 minutes)**
OPTION A
*(If you chose Option A under "Telling the Story" above, you may want to choose the following exercise for this segment.)*
Begin by asking the youth if they have heard this psalm before. Were certain phrases or words familiar to them? Were any of the ideas or images familiar? Perhaps some portion of the story reminded them of another story or song of Creation. Invite the youth to share the notes they made while the psalm was being read. Some youth may be reminded of a story or song that is unfamiliar to you. Allow each volunteer the opportunity to speak. Be sensitive to the fact that some youth may have been hearing the words from this passage for the first time.

Ask the youth if they were familiar with the song "How Majestic Is Your Name!" Did they enjoy listening to it? Encourage youth to compare and contrast Psalm 8 with the recording by referring to their notes. How were they alike? How were they different? What feelings did they have when listening to the song?

OPTION B
*(If you chose Option B under "Telling the Story" above, you may want to choose the following exercise for this segment.)*
Begin by asking the youth if they were able to create mental pictures for themselves as they listened to the story. You might encourage them to share their thoughts by asking questions such as:
■ What do human beings made "a little lower than God" (verse 5) look like?
■ What does "crowned with glory and honor" (verse 5) look like?
■ What do "the works of your [God's] hands" (verse 6) look like?
■ Could you see the heavens filled with the moon and stars?
■ Could you see the creatures of God's world, such as sheep, oxen, birds, or fish?

The interpretations and images of the youth may differ greatly from yours and from the others in the class. Be open to their reactions. Allow each youth the opportunity to speak.

Invite youth to share their sketches of Creation with the group. Some youth may be reluctant to show their artwork to others. Be sensitive to their needs, encouraging all youth to participate in whatever way they feel comfortable.

## Connecting to the Story (15–20 minutes)
OPTION A
*Needed: writing utensils, "My Psalm" handouts*
Suggest that the youth gather around a table and be seated for this activity in order for them to be able

to write more easily. Invite the youth to reflect upon today's Bible story, Psalm 8. Explain that the dictionary defines a psalm as a sacred song or hymn. Ask questions such as:
■ Where do you hear hymns most often?
■ What are some hymns that you are familiar with?
■ What is one of your favorite hymns?
■ What makes a song sacred?
■ What is this particular psalm about?

The youth will probably come up with several ideas. Allow each youth the opportunity to speak.

Give each youth a writing utensil and a copy of the handout "My Psalm." Invite the youth to write their own psalm. Remind them that this psalm is their own creation and does not have to rhyme or have a set length. Encourage youth to have fun and be creative. Some youth may have difficulty putting their thoughts of celebration or praise into words; be sensitive to their needs. Allow time for the youth to finish writing.

Encourage the learners to share their psalm with the group. When you have finished hearing from each volunteer, thank the entire group for participating.

OPTION B
*Needed: Bibles for each youth, newsprint and marker*
Begin this session by giving a Bible to each youth. Invite the youth to look at verses 4-6 of Psalm 8 with you. You may wish to have a student read the passage aloud. When the reading is completed, ask the following questions:

■ What does this passage have to say about humans' relationship with God?

■ Do you feel honored by God?

■ What does this passage have to say about humans' relationship with the rest of God's creation?

■ Do you feel a responsibility to care for God's creation?

■ What are some ways we can care for God's creation?

Encourage youth to call out their suggestions while you write them on the newsprint. They may have thoughts about conservation, pollution, animal rights, etc. Be open to their responses and allow each volunteer the opportunity to speak. Encourage youth to remember this list and put into practice their earth stewardship ideas.

### Exploring the Story (15–20 minutes)
OPTION A
*Needed: writing utensils, paper, Bibles, commentaries, Bible dictionaries*
Encourage youth to explore today's Bible story more deeply. Point out the various resources that you have gathered to aid in this exploration. Briefly describe how each resource might be used. For example, commentaries explain how others have interpreted the story or a particular portion of it, while a Bible dictionary defines specific concepts or elements in the story as they relate to their ancient time period.

Invite youth to discover more about the Book of Psalms. You may do this by asking the following questions:

■ What is a psalm?

■ Why were the psalms written?

■ How were they used?

■ Who wrote them?

■ What are the five books or sections of Psalms?

■ What are the categories of psalms?

You may wish to ask youth to work with a partner for this exercise. As the youth finish their explorations, you may want to gather as a group and invite them to share their discoveries.

OPTION B
*Needed: writing utensils, paper, "God's Creation" handouts, Bibles, Bible study helps*
Suggest that the youth be seated around a table for this activity in order for them to be able to write more easily. Distribute a Bible, writing utensil, and a copy of the handout "God's Creation" to each youth. Place the additional Bible study resources within easy reach of each youth.

Ask youth to look at the story of Creation in Psalm 8. Notice the different parts of creation that are listed, such as the moon and the stars, human beings, sheep and oxen, and birds and fish. Notice that God has given human beings dominion. (You may need to help youth define *dominion*. You might use a Bible dictionary and look up the word together.) Explain to the youth that the story of Creation is also told in Genesis 1. Ask youth to find Genesis 1 in their Bibles and then using the handout "God's Creation," invite youth to compare the two stories.

Allow enough time for youth to finish their explorations and complete the handout. When they have finished their study, encourage youth to share their responses with the rest of the group.

**Living the Story
(5–10 minutes)**
*OPTION A*
Invite your youth to stand in a circle with you and hold hands. Ask them to think silently about something they celebrate and are thankful for in their own lives. Tell the group that you will be leading them in a responsive prayer of praise. Explain that you will invite them to share their thanksgiving with the group one at a time. As each youth finishes speaking, the entire group will respond in unison with "O Lord, how majestic is your name!"

Allow a few moments of silence for youth to reflect upon their blessings. Then begin sharing these aloud one at a time, followed by the sentence "O Lord, how majestic is your name!"

Some youth may be eager to share, while others might be more reluctant. Be sensitive to the needs of the individuals in the group. When everyone has had an opportunity to participate, close the session with a resounding "Amen!"

OPTION B
*Needed: chalkboard and chalk or newsprint and marker, cassette or CD player, recording of the song "How Majestic Is Your Name!" (optional)*
To close this session, ask the youth to recall that Psalm 8 is a psalm of celebration and praise. Invite them to think of something they celebrate and are thankful for in their own

lives. You may wish to play the song "How Majestic Is Your Name!" If so, start the recording and, while it is playing, allow time for the youth to reflect. When the recording is finished, encourage youth to come forward and write their thanksgiving on the chalkboard or on newsprint.

The youth may write a variety of responses. Be open to their ideas, allowing time for each youth to participate who feels comfortable doing so.

As volunteers conclude their writing, encourage your youth to gather in a circle with you. Thank them all for being present today and for their great participation. You may wish to lead the youth in a closing prayer of praise, thanking God for the blessings they have listed either on chalkboard or newsprint.

**Things to Ponder**
As always, there may be youth who feel they have nothing about which to be thankful. Indeed, some youth have difficult lives. However, it is an exercise in faith to be able to find something to be thankful for even in the midst of our difficulties. Encourage youth who you sense may be having these struggles. Schedule times to meet with them apart from class to share in their struggles and to help them find hope.

**Looking Ahead**
For the next session, you may need to find a video depiction of the story of the feeding of the five thousand. You may also want to make a videotape of a faith healing on a televangelism show for use during the session.

# My Psalm

 God's Creation

*Compare the descriptions of Creation found in Psalm 8 with the story of Creation found in Genesis 1. On what day were the moon and stars created? The animals? What do the stories say about human beings? Look for similarities and differences.*

**Psalm 8**                    **Genesis 1**

# 17. Feeding the Five Thousand

*Bible Story: John 6:1-15*

Carol S. Adams

## A Story behind the Story

Once again we come to what may be a familiar story to many. Yet there is so much more to the story that learners may discover. Review the parallel accounts of this story for more insight (Matthew 14:13-21; Mark 6:32-44; Luke 9:10-17). This is the only parable of Jesus' that is recorded in all four of the Gospels.

The story of the "feeding of the five thousand," as it is often referred to, appears among other stories of Jesus healing and performing miracles. At this point in John we see that Jesus has turned water into wine, healed an official's son, and healed people with disabilities at a pool. Yet John's Gospel has a unique flavor to it. The author focuses less on the events of Jesus and more on the meanings of those events. John draws in several testimonies about Jesus. He writes of John the Baptist's testimony (John 3:22-30; 5:33-36), Jesus' own testimony (5:31), the Father's testimony (5:36-38), and the testimony of Scripture (5:39-40). He draws the reader away from dwelling on the events and the facts; rather, he challenges the reader to think about the profound meanings that lie within.

So, what deep meaning can we find in this apparently simple story about eating a picnic lunch?

Some scholars agree that Jesus was not even intending to feed the people a meal. He was speaking allegorically when he asked Philip about finding bread for everyone. He was talking about the need to feed their souls, which was the nature of his ministry. Many Jews believed that the Messiah would bring the miraculous manna that their ancestors had eaten under Moses. Yet Jesus pointed to a better "meal"—himself. The disciples quickly responded to the literal meaning, and Jesus chose to use that as well.

Other scholars agree that Jesus had intended to feed their bodies all along. This demonstrates his great care for our every need, both spiritually and physically. The people were in need, and Jesus could fulfill that need. Jesus' act of feeding the people's physical bodies also confirms his ability to use everything for the glory of God.

As you can see, there are many ways to experience and understand this rich story. Through this session, the youth of your class (and you as well) will have an opportunity to plumb the depths of its multilayered meaning.

## Enter the Story

Try waiting until you are quite hungry to read this story, then having a snack or meal, and reading it again when satisfied. Did you have a different perspective on it, depending on how full your stomach was? Consider how someone who lives in poverty or famine might understand this story versus someone who lives in wealth and abundance. Pray that God might open your mind to the message this story might have for you.

## POSSIBLE YOUTH CONTACT POINTS

- How do I find courage to step out in faith?
- How do I respond when God moves in miraculous ways?

## YOU MAY NEED

- cookie or doughnut
- snacks
- *The Message* or other contemporary Bible paraphrase
- Bibles
- video depicting the feeding of the five thousand
- VCR and TV
- video clip of faith healings from a television ministry (optional)
- "It's Feeding Time!" handouts
- writing utensils
- "The Passover Feast" handouts
- Bible study helps, such as Bible dictionaries, concordances, commentaries, and Bible encyclopedias
- index cards
- candle
- matches or lighter

## Setting the Stage (5–10 minutes)

OPTION A

*Needed: cookie or doughnut (or other favorite treat)*

As students arrive, ask them if anyone would like a cookie, doughnut, or whatever treat you have accessible. Don't show them the treat yet; keep it hidden away. Merely take orders and find out who is interested in having some.

When all have arrived and settled in, take a final count of those desiring a treat. Bring out the special treat. Inform the group that you are confident there is enough available for every person to have some. Proceed by breaking the treat into the necessary number of pieces. Distribute and enjoy.

Take note of people's reactions. Do some refuse the piece because it is too small? Is there grumbling when they discover there is only one treat to be shared by all? Make a mental note of the reactions for use in later discussions.

OPTION B

*Needed: snacks*

As students arrive, have snacks available for them to munch on. Encourage everyone to grab a bite before you begin.

Gather the group and begin the following discussion: *Have you ever gone on a day trip where you needed to pack a lunch?* Perhaps it was an outdoor concert, a hike, or a sports tournament. Have your own example ready to share to get them started. Then invite learners to share stories of such times. Ask: *Was there ever a time when you had such an event and you forgot your lunch? If so, what did you do?*

*Did you buy an expensive lunch from the vendors? Mooch off those around you? Go hungry, often getting distracted by your growling stomach?* Invite more sharing, perhaps in partners or groups.

Ask the learners if they have ever been hungry during some important event, such as a test, a performance, etc. How did this affect the event?

Say: *Today's lesson involves hungry people. Let's see what happens.*

## Telling the Story (5–10 minutes)

OPTION A

*Needed:* The Message *or other contemporary Bible paraphrase,* Bibles

Gather the learners for a story. Allow them to finish their snacks as long as it is not distracting to others in the group. Invite them to close their eyes as they listen to the story. Encourage them to picture the story as if it were happening to them. They can put themselves in the place of any of the characters.

Pull out your copy of *The Message* or other contemporary Bible paraphrase. Read John 6:1-15 aloud.

Next, have learners retrieve their own Bibles. As a group, turn to John 6:1-15. Invite someone to read the story aloud from his or her Bible. Encourage several to read, if many versions are represented in your group. Discuss similarities and differences among the translations or between the translations and the contemporary paraphrase.

- Which was easier to understand?
- Were there differences in specific words?
- Does this make any difference to the meaning of the phrase or story in general?

OPTION B

*Needed: videos, TV and VCR*

Before the session, gather one or more videos that include a depiction of the miracle of Jesus feeding the five thousand. You may choose a realistic representation, such as in the movie *Jesus* (available from Campus Crusade for Christ International at 407/826-2000). Or you might find it fun to show a version from a children's video.

Inform the group that today you will get to see one of Jesus' miracles. Show as many videos as you have decided upon. Gather feedback from the viewers. Did it seem believable or realistic? Compare and contrast versions if you show more than one video.

Have the learners open their Bibles to the John passage. Invite a volunteer to read the passage aloud. If more than one version is available, have those read as well. Compare the readings with the video versions. How were they similar or different?

Ask the group to imagine they were filming their own version of the story.
- How would your video look?
- What angle would you take?
- Who would the actors be?
- Where would you do the filming?
- Would you take a realistic approach or a more creative or metaphorical approach?

## Reacting to the Story (15–20 minutes)

OPTION A

Invite learners to reflect upon the story. Perhaps read it out loud one more time. Invite discussion using these suggestions:
- Do you think this story really happened? Why or why not?

- How do you think the loaves and fish became available for Jesus to use? Did the boy volunteer them? Did the disciples ask the boy if they could use them? Did they go to the boy telling him that Jesus asked if they could share his food? How else might it have happened?
- How would you have reacted if you were there when the miracle occurred?
- How might this experience have changed the multitude's perceptions of Jesus?
- How might this experience have changed the disciples' perceptions of Jesus?

Invite the youth to imagine that one of their best friends or a family member was present for the miracle. Then ask:
- When the person came and told you about it, how would you have responded?
- Would you have been skeptical? Why or why not?
- What questions would you have asked?
- What could this person have said or done to help you believe it really happened?
- Would it be helpful to go to the place where it occurred?

OPTION B

Invite the learners to put themselves in the place of the disciples in this story. Take time to discuss the story from the disciples' perspectives.
- What might they have been thinking or feeling?
- Do you think they grumbled at the thought of feeding so many people?
- Did different disciples respond differently, perhaps even bringing dissension into the group?

Brainstorm all the possible reactions they may have had.

After the brainstorming, lead a discussion about how the disciples thought, felt, and responded in each situation:
- when they saw so many people gathered
- when Jesus asked them about feeding the multitude
- when Jesus asked them to have everyone sit down
- when Jesus blessed the food and it was distributed
- when Jesus asked them to gather the leftover food
- when so much leftover food was collected

Wrap up this segment by posing a couple more questions about the disciples' perspective.
- Do you think the disciples were hungry too? Did they get to eat along with the others?
- How might this experience have changed the disciples' perceptions of Jesus?

## Connecting to the Story (15–20 minutes)
OPTION A

Share a story about a time in your life when someone in authority asked you to do something that seemed unbelievable, yet when you trusted the authority figure and completed the task, it all worked out. Perhaps a coach asked you to try a play that seemed like it would not work, yet when you and your teammates tried it, it worked every time. Or perhaps an art teacher showed you a new technique that you were doubtful about, but once you tried it yourself, you discovered it produced amazing results.

After sharing your story, invite the learners to think of their own stories of the same sort, perhaps involving a coach, a teacher, or a parent. You may need to give them a few moments to think of one. As soon as someone is ready to tell a story, let him or her go. Then, after each story, ask the storyteller to clarify his or her responses.
- How did you respond to the initial request?
- How did you respond after trying it and finding that it worked?
- How did the outcome change your view of the person who made the original request?

Point out that sometimes we experience things that may shake up our beliefs and how we view the world.

## OPTION B
*Needed: video clip of faith healings (optional), TV and VCR*
Ask the learners to share stories they have seen or heard where God was at work. Perhaps some are unbelievable stories of healing or someone's claim to have heard God speaking to them. Encourage them to share stories they have heard that may be a stretch to believe as well as some more realistic stories. It would not be unusual for your students to mention shows on TV in which people claim to be healed. You may even want to show a clip from such a show if one is available.

After several students have shared, encourage discussion using questions such as the following:
- What makes some of these stories so unbelievable?
- Does the believability depend upon who is telling the story? Why or why not?

- How could you know for sure that it was true?
- If such an event happened to you, how would that change how you respond when others tell you unbelievable stories?
- We read of many miracles in the Bible. Do these things still happen today? How do we know?

If the discussion goes long, ask the learners to share more stories with you after the session. This postponement of the discussion will allow you to transition to the next section on schedule.

## Exploring the Story (15–20 minutes)

OPTION A

*Needed: "It's Feeding Time!" handouts, writing utensils, Bibles*

Pass out the handouts entitled "It's Feeding Time!" and writing utensils. Point out (or have a volunteer read) the sentence about how the feeding of the five thousand is the only miracle of Jesus that is recorded in all four of the Gospels. Invite responses as to why it would be included in all four Gospels when others stories were not. Have volunteers read these different accounts aloud:
- Matthew 14:13-21
- Mark 6:32-44
- Luke 9:10-17
- John 6:1-15

Following the outline on the handout, have each person list the points that all four stories have in common. Also have them list the differences among the four versions. And then, after all have had a chance to write their responses, invite sharing. Again, this may be done first with partners or small groups and then as a whole group.

Move to the final question on the handout: *Which version is most appealing to you? Why?* Encourage everyone to share their response. Remind them that there are no right or wrong answers to this question. Everyone's opinion is valid.

OPTION B

*Needed: "The Passover Feast" handouts, Bibles, Bible study helps*

Before the session, gather several reference tools that might contain information regarding the Passover Feast. Bible dictionaries or commentaries may be helpful. You may also gather books about Jewish festivals or perhaps even search on the Internet.

Give each learner a copy of the handout entitled "The Passover Feast." John's account of this miracle states that the Passover Feast was at hand. Why might this have been significant? What can we find out about the Passover Feast?

Point out the reference tools that you have available. Encourage your youth to work in groups to find out as much information about the Passover as they can. Instruct them to write several ideas on their work sheets. Some things they might want to look for include the following:
- What is the history of the Passover celebration? Why is it celebrated?
- What happens at Passover? How do the Jews celebrate it?
- Why would this festival have been significant for John to mention in his account of the miracle?

After all have had a chance to use the reference tools, discuss what they discovered. See if you can all agree upon a reason why John felt it necessary to mention the feast while the other Gospel writers did not. It may be helpful to study more about each Gospel writer and the angle each took in writing his Gospel. Many study Bibles have adequate introduction and background sections that may be helpful.

### Living the Story
### (5–10 minutes)
OPTION A

*Needed: index cards, writing utensils, candle, matches or lighter*
If you chose this option for the previous lesson, remind the learners of this ritual time of commitment. Gather the group together and instruct them to sit on the floor in a circle. Place the candle in the center and light it. Invite the group to reflect back over the lesson. Review the key discussion points of the lesson: the disciples' perspective of the story, God working in miraculous ways, etc.

Tell the group that now has come the time of commitment for each one of them. Pass out index cards and writing utensils. Ask them to write down one or two things they will commit to as a result of studying this lesson. Some possible commitments might be:
■ I will be open to God working in miraculous ways.
■ I will study to gain more of a disciple's perspective.

Encourage them to take a general commitment (such as the ones listed) and come up with at least one specific way to live it out.

After all have written their commitments, close in a prayer. Invite learners to pray silently or out loud, asking for God's help in carrying out their commitments.

OPTION B
Invite the learners to sit in a circle. If appropriate, remind them of the stories shared in Option A under "Connecting to the Story." These were the stories about them being surprised that an authority figure's instruction worked out. Challenge the students to think about how they respond when they know God wants them to do something in particular.
■ Are you reluctant because it seems impossible or unbelievable?
■ Is it easy to brush God's request aside because you cannot see God like you can another authority figure?

Give the learners a few moments to examine their responses to God. Encourage a silent time of reflection. Challenge the learners to make commitments to step out in faith the next time they sense God leading them to do things. Challenge them to courageously step out and expect God to do amazing things. Close in a prayer of commitment.

### Things to Ponder
Once again, take some time to evaluate how the session went. Were the learners able to project themselves into the story? What questions arose? How can you address these questions at another time? Note also how many of them have been exposed to God working in miraculous ways in people's lives. Many youth have limited exposure to such things. Others may not be open at all to such thoughts. Assess where your group stands. Follow up with any youth who seemed either interested or troubled by the discussion.

# It's Feeding Time!

*The feeding of the five thousand is the only miracle of Jesus that is recorded in all four of the Gospels. Check it out!*

- **Matthew 14:13-21**
- **Mark 6:32-44**
- **Luke 9:10-17**
- **John 6:1-15**

List the points that all four stories have in common.

List the differences among the four versions.

What version is most appealing to you? Why?

# The Passover Feast

*John 6:4 states that the Passover Feast was at hand. Using Bible reference tools, such as a Bible dictionary, let's explore all we can about this feast.*

What is the history of the Passover celebration? Why is it celebrated?

What happens at Passover? How do the Jews celebrate it?

Why would this have been significant for John to mention in his account of the miracle?

# BibleQuest Bookmark Stories Index

| Year I | BookMarks Story | Title | Corresponding Lesson |
|---|---|---|---|
| Fall | Genesis 1:1–2:4a | Creation | Vol. 3, Lesson 1 |
| | Exodus 3:1-12 | The Burning Bush | Vol. 1, Lesson 10 |
| | 1 Samuel 16:1-13 | David Chosen King | Vol. 6, Lesson 1 |
| | Isaiah 11:1-9 | Peaceable Kingdom | Vol. 1, Lesson 13 |
| Winter | Matthew 1:18-24 | Joseph's Dream | Vol. 1, Lesson 16 |
| | Mark 1:1-11 | Jesus' Baptism | Vol. 6, Lesson 2 |
| Spring | John 20:1-18 | Women at the Tomb | Vol. 6, Lesson 3 |
| | Revelation 21:1-7 | God Always with Us | Vol. 6, Lesson 4 |
| Summer | Psalm 150 | A Psalm of Praise | Vol. 6, Lesson 5 |
| | Psalm 23 | Shepherd Psalm | Vol. 4, Lesson 2 |
| | Luke 10:38–11:4 | Prayer Jesus Taught | Vol. 6, Lesson 6 |

| Year 2 | Bookmarks Story | Title | Corresponding Lesson |
|---|---|---|---|
| Fall | Genesis 2:4b-25 | Creation | Vol. 6, Lesson 7 |
| | Genesis 7–8 | Noah | Vol. 6, Lesson 8 |
| | Genesis 17:1-27 | Abraham and Sarah | Vol. 1, Lesson 2 |
| | Exodus 20:1-21 | Ten Commandments | Vol. 6, Lesson 9 |
| Winter | Ruth 1–4 | Ruth | Vol. 2, Lesson 3 |
| | 2 Samuel 7:1-17 | Covenant with David | Vol. 4, Lesson 1 |
| | 2 Kings 22 | Josiah and Huldah | Vol. 6, Lesson 10 |
| | Jeremiah 31:31-34 | Jeremiah | Vol. 6, Lesson 11 |
| Spring | Mark 2:23-28 | Jesus and the Sabbath | Vol. 6, Lesson 12 |
| | Luke 24:13-35 | Emmaus Road | Vol. 6, Lesson 13 |
| | Acts 2 | Pentecost | Vol. 4, Lesson 13 |
| | Hebrews 11:1–12:2 | Cloud of Witnesses | Vol. 6, Lesson 14 |
| Summer | Psalm 105 | God's Faithfulness | Vol. 6, Lesson 15 |
| | Psalm 8 | Psalm of Creation | Vol. 6, Lesson 16 |
| | John 6:1-14 | Feeding the 5,000 | Vol. 6, Lesson 17 |

| Year 3 | Bookmarks Story | Title | Corresponding Lesson |
|---|---|---|---|
| Fall | Genesis 18:1-15 | Welcome Strangers | Vol. 5, Lesson 1 |
| | Exodus 2:1-12; 12–14 | Exodus | Vol. 1, Lesson 9 |
| | 2 Kings 4:1-37 | Elisha and the Widow's Oil | Vol. 5, Lesson 2 |
| | Micah 4:1-8 | Reign of God | Vol. 5, Lesson 3 |

| **Year 3** (cont.) | **Bookmarks Story** | **Title** | **Corresponding Lesson** |
|---|---|---|---|
| Winter | Luke 1:39-56 | Mary's Song | Vol. 3, Lesson 13 |
| | Luke 4:16-30 | Jesus' Announcement | Vol. 2, Lesson 5 |
| | Luke 10:25-37 | The Good Samaritan | Vol. 2, Lesson 4 |
| | Luke 16:19-31 | Rich Man and Lazarus | Vol. 3, Lesson 7 |
| Spring | Matthew 20:20-28 | Seeking Honor | Vol. 5, Lesson 4 |
| | Matthew 22:34-40 | Great Commandment | Vol. 5, Lesson 5 |
| | Matthew 25:31-46 | The Least of These | Vol. 2, Lesson 8 |
| | Philemon | Onesimus | Vol. 5, Lesson 6 |
| Summer | Jeremiah 18:1-6 | The Potter's Wheel | Vol. 5, Lesson 7 |
| | Matthew 4:23–5:16 | Sermon on the Mount | Vol. 5, Lesson 8 |
| | James 1:22–2:26 | Doers, Not Just Hearers | Vol. 5, Lesson 9 |

| **Year 4** | **Bookmarks Story** | **Title** | **Corresponding Lesson** |
|---|---|---|---|
| Fall | Genesis 3 | Problems in the Garden | Vol. 1, Lesson 1 |
| | Genesis 39:1-3; 45:1–46:7 | Joseph | Vol. 5, Lesson 10 |
| | Joshua 3–4 | Joshua | Vol. 5, Lesson 11 |
| | 1 Samuel 25 | Abigail | Vol. 5, Lesson 12 |
| Winter | Jonah 1–4 | Jonah | Vol. 5, Lesson 13 |
| | Luke 2:25-38 | Simeon and Anna | Vol. 5, Lesson 14 |
| | John 3:1-21 | Nicodemus | Vol. 1, Lesson 5 |
| | Luke 19:1-10 | Zacchaeus | Vol. 1, Lesson 8 |
| Spring | Mark 14:3-9 | Anointing at Bethany | Vol. 5, Lesson 15 |
| | John 20:19-29 | Thomas Hears Good News | Vol. 5, Lesson 16 |
| | Acts 9:1-19a | Saul's Conversion | Vol. 4, Lesson 15 |
| | Acts 16:11-40 | Lydia; Paul and Silas in Prison | Vol. 5, Lesson 17 |
| Summer | Daniel 6:6-23 | Daniel in Lion's Den | Vol. 4, Lesson 3 |
| | Luke 14:15-24 | Great Banquet | Vol. 5, Lesson 18 |
| | Revelation 7:9-17 | Every Nation | Vol. 5, Lesson 19 |